PAPER
magic

PAPER
magic

JANE GORDON-CLARK

Pantheon Books, New York

To C.S.G.C.

Conceived, edited and designed by Frances Lincoln Limited,
Apollo Works, 5 Charlton Kings Road, London NW5 2SB, England

Library of Congress Cataloging-in-Publication Data
Gordon-Clark, Jane.
    Paper magic/by Jane Gordon-Clark.
        p.   cm.
    Includes bibliographical references and index.
    ISBN 0-679-40404-X
        1. Paper-hanging – Amateurs' manuals. 2. Wallpaper – Amateurs'
    manuals. 3. Interior decoration – Amateurs' manuals. I. Title.
    TH8423.G67   1991
    698'.6—dc20   90-27836
                                                                    CIP

Printed and bound in Hong Kong by Kwong Fat Offset Printing Co Ltd
First American edition

CONTENTS

INTRODUCTION

Wallpaper is unique in its potential for giving an interior a high degree of finish, at the same time creating a mood and reflecting the taste and personality of the occupants. The combination of colour and pattern in a pleasing design will lift the spirit: a beautiful paper will give pleasure every time you enter a room or open the front door, and greet guests with a far more positive welcome than that offered by a painted wall.

The two principal alternatives to wallpaper in decoration are fabric and paint, but both have limitations. Fabric stretched on walls offers a luxurious richness of texture and design but is not as versatile in its application as paper; it is more complicated to hang and less practical *in situ* because of dust. Paint is a popular decorating option, since it is relatively undemanding and inexpensive, but even when more ambitious textured effects break the surface of the wall and give it some depth by reflecting light, the result is no more than to coat the room's shell with a covering of colour. Paint can seem dull in comparison with the wonderful opportunities presented by wallpaper.

Of course wallpaper too can be bland. The challenge is first to make a discriminating choice from the range of papers available, which include many exciting but little-known designs from makers who are not necessarily household names. Second, it needs to be displayed to best effect, in a way that suits the setting but also makes a distinctive and perhaps intriguing statement. Wallpaper in this book is far from a byword for some mindless utilitarian patterned cover-up. It is a positive force in decorating.

WALLPAPER PRINTING

Some of the milestones in papermaking and printing have had a telling effect on wallpaper's appearance and impact; others have simply streamlined aspects of the production process. But while up-to-date machines may explore new effects made possible by technological discoveries, manufacturers still take pains to imitate the mellower appearance of outmoded printing techniques. Indeed, some of today's finest and most expensive papers are still actually hand-printed – often from original blocks.

The earliest western wallpapers were all block-printed, and the process has continued to be used since the sixteenth century. Hand-blocked papers today are easily recognized by their rich, chalky, slightly sticky colour, which forms into a vague outline around the printed area when the block is lifted. Slight irregularities in the register of different colours add to the charm and appeal of hand-made designs, making machine-printed papers seem flat and mechanical in comparison.

The hand-blocking process today is much as it was in the past. Designs are cut on blocks of seasoned hardwood and printed one colour at a time.

The spectacular Réveillon wallpaper decorating the hallway of the Phelps-Hatheway House in Connecticut was imported from France in 1794. It incorporates favourite neo-classical devices inspired by the Roman wall paintings excavated at Herculaneum and Pompeii. Such rich colouring and intricate designs surprise people accustomed to the blander tones and repetitive style of many modern wallpapers.

A reinterpretation of the same paper (BELOW) is produced by screen-printing rather than the original hand-blocking technique.

Printing wallpaper by hand using carved wooden blocks is a slow and painstaking process. Each colour is applied separately along a length of paper and allowed to dry before the next is printed, using a different block. Here the last of seven colours is being printed on 'Gothic Lily', a wallpaper designed by A.W.N. Pugin for the Palace of Westminster in the nineteenth century (see also pages 46 and 51). Each roll of this paper takes about five days to complete.

The techniques for block-printing are essentially the same today as they have been for the last two centuries and, indeed, many of the original woodblocks are still in use. The time and skill required to produce these fine papers results in a considerably more expensive product than machine-made wallpapers. Yet a glimpse of the superb quality and rich, dense colours achieved by the hand process should convince anyone of the distinction that these papers bring to the decoration of the walls.

Each colour requires a different block, and some papers need large numbers of blocks to complete their design. The fact that original blocks are still sometimes available makes reprinting these old document papers a viable economic practicality today: creating new blocks makes these already costly papers prohibitively expensive.

In printing the paper is fed in a continuous roll over a padded table. The block is dipped in a tray of colour and moved across to the printing table to be lowered and pressed with a lever onto the paper's surface. The whole roll is printed with the first colour and dried before the next can be started: a tiny pin at the corner of the block makes a register mark so that subsequent colours are printed in the right place.

For more than two hundred years wallpaper makers printed only by means of blocks, refining the quality and complexity of their designs and perfecting the use of many different colours to achieve papers of extraordinary sophistication.

It was the advent of 'endless paper' produced by the roll instead of the sheet, that allowed wallpaper to be machine-printed. By the 1840s patterns were being transferred to the paper by means of an engraved copper cylinder or rollers with a design raised on the surface. The technique of printing designs in several colours quickly followed. Other machines had rollers capable of moulding and embossing paper, and soon this could be done in a single process, with elements of the design standing out in relief.

Pride in sheer technical prowess eclipsed design merit in many Victorian wallpapers, which celebrated the possibility of using anything up to eight colours all too gaudily. The revolt against this by the Arts and Crafts Movement is famous and because of it arbiters of taste can still sound slightly apologetic when writing about machine-printed wallpaper. But machine-printing brought the undoubted advantage of a lower price which vastly expanded the market for wallpaper, making it possible for every household to afford papers of high design quality to decorate their walls in the latter part of the century.

The late Victorian design renaissance breathed new life into the art of block-printing and some of the blocks made by companies like Morris & Co still exist and are in use.

Later designs by William Shand Kydd and Arthur Silver drew on hand-printing techniques such as stencilling which is still occasionally used for hand-made wallpapers today. For hand-printed paper, screen-printing is more widespread nowadays than block-printing. Again the process is lengthy and painstaking, with the colours laid on one at a time, and a separate screen needed for each. The main advantage of screen-printing lies in its ability to reproduce the fluidity and spontaneity of the artist's brushstrokes very accurately. The ink may be laid on thickly for a rich painterly effect, it can be brushed across the surface in the merest whisper of colour – or it can reflect any degree of subtlety in between.

Modern manufacturing techniques have made a variety of often very high quality papers widely available. But perhaps the greatest accolade to the vigour and beauty of block-printing, screen-printing and stencilling is that many modern techniques seek to emulate their traditional hand-crafted beauty.

THE RENAISSANCE OF WALLPAPER

For some decades wallpaper has been the sleeping beauty of good decorating, and little creative imagination has gone into its design. The common impression is of huge quantities of relatively undistinguished mass-produced papers – repetitive in design concept, inconsequential in colouring and above all cheap – to be picked up in chain stores and DIY hypermarkets. These cover the walls, concealing bumps and cracks with a neat, clean finish, but never add that extra dimension of style and panache that an interesting wallpaper can contribute to the decoration of a room.

However, some specialist wallpaper companies have been leading the way out of this thicket with interesting and unusual ideas. Sometimes hand-printed and produced on a small scale, the pick of these papers can be expensive, but creative inspiration has a way of working through all levels of the market. Just as *haute couture* springs from the great Paris fashion houses and filters down in essence to influence firms mass-producing clothing for the high street, so modern design and innovation in wallpaper will gradually appear at generally accessible price levels – and, it is hoped, will meanwhile improve the quality of the mass-manufactured product. Good design, as opposed to quality of materials and production, need not necessarily be more expensive than uninspiring design.

Yet people who expect to pay large sums for carpets and soft-furnishing or window treatments often feel quite shocked when they see the high cost of hand-printed wallpapers. Somehow everyone expects wallpapers to be cheap. But beautiful craftsmanship is and should be expensive. Allied to excellence in design it imparts a quality of particular distinction and character to a room far more positively than wall-to-wall carpeting or lined, swagged and trimmed curtains.

While a handful of original ideas are being developed by imaginative designers today, probably more characteristic of current style is the trend for documentary wallpapers and fabrics. They are produced – accurately or otherwise – as copies of old papers, and some lovely period designs result. These can be used to breathe a reminder of a past age into our interiors – just a hint to be developed in furnishings and upholstery – or as a full-scale attempt at authenticity. Some papers are produced in updated colourways, others are in their original colours. It is up to you to select the degree of accuracy that you and the room demand. But choosing a paper of suitable style for the age of the room is not the only way to use these archive papers; they look equally effective in a modern setting where they may not even appear to be historic reproductions – which is part of the fun of an open-minded juxtaposition of time and ideas.

The effects of different printing techniques. From top to bottom: block-printing, screen-printing, machine-printing and hand-stencilling.

THE MAGIC
OF PAPER

TROMPE L'OEIL EFFECTS

Since its earliest beginnings in Europe, wallpaper has been produced in imitation of other, more expensive wall finishes and furnishings. The chameleon capacity of paper to disguise itself is a ceaseless source of wonder and delight. Paper can physically assume a third dimension by being coated with textured finishes or by various processes of embossing. But flat paper can take on an equally convincing illusionist character by being painted or printed with colours and patterns that deceive the eye with their simulation of light and shadow. The range of dramatic, beautiful and witty effects created by the papermaker's art in the past continues to offer inspiration and the chance to be enterprising and original in decorating homes today. Totally different in concept from the stylized designs and cool abstraction of the flat repeating patterns, these papers bring the excitement of the unexpected, a touch of magic, and a flash of wit to the enjoyment of decoration.

WALLHANGINGS OF TAPESTRY & LEATHER

The pictorial tapestries and stamped leather hangings that rank among the antecedents of wallpapers once decorated interiors very remote from those most of us inhabit today. But from the first these materials inspired wallpaper makers, and it is interesting to trace some of the ways in which this inspiration has been reinterpreted over the years.

Tapestries have always been among the rarest and most costly furnishings and wallpapers have been inspired both by their imagery and by their texture. The rich verdure colours and woven effects of the old tapestries used as wallhangings have been wonderfully re-created in fine wallpaper. Few of us have the opportunity of hanging the kind of wallpaper that is a perfect imitation of a grand tapestry, but some tapestry effects can be translated into an up-to-date context. Papers with embossed stitched effects have something of the properties of fabric in softening an interior. The cocoon-like atmosphere evoked by their woven textures could be very appropriate in a winter room warmed by a roaring log fire for instance, or on the walls of a study or dining room. There is inspiration also in the way in which tapestry papers became popular for hallways and dining rooms in some homes at the turn of this century, where they harmonized with the fashion for neo-Jacobean furniture and stained oak woodwork.

The effects possible from various simulations of stamped leather tend to be more grandiose, less domestic in atmosphere. Long before the invention of wallpaper, embossed and gilded leather was esteemed for wallhangings as well as in various forms of upholstery. The techniques

LEFT *'Fontainebleau' wallpaper reprinted by Zuber from a nineteenth-century design achieves a remarkably realistic imitation of the thickly woven texture of tapestry.*

PREVIOUS PAGE *Seen from a distance, the carefully graded tones and colours in this wallpaper form three-dimensional highlights and shadows. It gives a convincing impression of a sprigged chintz fabric catching the light as it falls in gentle folds.*

RIGHT *The tapestry wallpaper shown on page 12 creates an atmosphere of baronial splendour in a New York apartment. It provides a fitting backdrop for a collection of antique furnishings, and proves that bold patterns work just as well in small modern rooms as in more spacious period interiors.*

BELOW *The drawing room of the Linley Sambourne House, a London terrace house which is the headquarters of the Victorian Society, still contains the original decorations and furniture dating from the latter part of the nineteenth century. The richly coloured wallpaper is typical of popular designs of the period imitating the effects of leatherwork, with embossed patterns printed on a gilded ground.*

had been brought by Arabs from Morocco to Cordoba in Spain, and by the late seventeenth century fine workmanship was being produced by craftsmen in England, France and the Low Countries. It was natural for the earliest wallpapers to imitate the look and finish of contemporary leather and to draw on many of the same designs, from baroque ornamentation to motifs inspired by the new craze for *Chinoiserie*. Many gilders easily turned their skills to making the new 'stampt' or 'imbost' papers, and some of their methods remained in use for years. A taste for authentic leather hangings persisted in parts of Europe through the eighteenth century so an inexpensive alternative was provided by these high-quality wallpapers simulating leather, with embossed motifs decorated with metal foil and lustrous effects achieved with powdered silicates such as mica and talc.

There was a resurgence of taste for leather-like finishes among the Victorians, particularly once the notion of dividing the wall into three sections had taken hold: embossed effects were felt to be particularly suited to the dado. From the 1860s Japanese 'leather paper' was imported into England and America and found its way into some grander houses. Although this paper was made by craftsmen in Japan, many of the highly embossed patterns were western in style, recalling the exuberance of Renaissance and baroque ornamentation of earlier wallpapers. As the fashion for things Japanese grew, some more Orientally inspired motifs appeared. In the late 1870s Lincrusta Walton, a new material based on solidified linseed oil, was patented. Lincrusta was capable of imitating relief plasterwork and carving as well as stamped leather, and was the first of many similar composition products which are usually classed as wallpapers. It was sold coloured, often with gilt ornamentation in typical leather fashion, or plain, to be painted or varnished *in situ*. The designs showed a typically Victorian gamut of influence: Celtic, Egyptian, Byzantine and Oriental. Lincrusta and its imitators were, of course, widely used for dados, where they sometimes survive. When we see them in old houses they usually look rather dull and brown, but this is often because the patina of the gilding has been lost, for they certainly started life as rich and lustrous as their seventeenth-century predecessors.

LUXURIOUS TEXTILES

One of the earliest and most enduring achievements of papermaking has been to imitate the textured effects of some of the most sumptuous fabrics. Cut velvet, with its relief figuring of downy pile, and damask-woven silks, in which a variation in the direction of the weave reflects light in areas of patterning, were originally textile masterpieces produced by Italian weavers of the Renaissance which only the richest households could afford. Ingenuity was applied to create less costly textile imitations for use as wall hangings. Indeed, when flock papers began to be produced in the seventeenth century, the craftsmen simply applied the established process for making mock velvet to paper instead of cloth.

Flock paper is made by printing or stencilling a design in an adhesive onto paper and then lightly brushing minute wool or silk shavings over it. The fibres stick to the pattern and the background is left clear. The resulting contrast between the slightly raised surface of the matt-textured flocking and the smooth ground looks very much like richly figured velvet. When hanging on a wall some original examples are so realistic that it is often hard to distinguish paper from fabric.

Flock papers have a long and grand pedigree, and it is sad that the image of flock has been tarnished for many of us by the uninspiring sight of modern cheap versions adorning the walls of bars and restaurants. Museum conservationists and the curators of grand historic houses regard fine flock papers with suitable deference and respect, and skilfully produced examples are among the most richly textured wallpapers to be found. Flock papers produced in London were highly esteemed and were exported to Europe and North America in the eighteenth century. Mme de Pompadour chose a blue flock to line her closet at Versailles and, of course, once the mistress of Louis XV had chosen it the fashion spread; walls and closets similarly papered were soon *de rigueur* in fashionable French society. Since flock wallpapers were valued and cared for, some have actually survived in the great houses to which they lent an additional aura of magnificence. Others are copied and replaced when period interiors are restored.

If you want to hang good-quality flock paper you can still buy it printed by hand to the original designs. Flock papers can look appropriate and attractive in any period environment with rooms of sufficient grandeur to accommodate them. This does not necessarily imply great size: many designers have successfully incorporated rich flock papers into quite small rooms, where they introduce a background

The flock wallpaper in this room at Rousham Park in Oxfordshire is hung on the upper part of the walls, above the panelled dado. A light coloured background contrasts with the deep red areas of patterning and enriches the effect of the flock.

RIGHT *Renaissance damasks and brocades have always been a source of inspiration for wallpapers. The impact of the stylized foliage depends not just on scale but on the degree of tone or colour contrast between figuring and ground. Some papers are designed to run fluently in continuous all-over patterns; others are based on motifs with a more static, majestic quality.*

BELOW *A collection of moiré-patterned papers of differing scales reflects some of the variety available in moiré designs, from very fine overall texturing or simple stripes to large-scale figuring (see also page 18).*

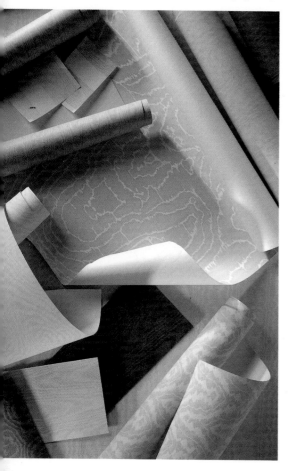

of great luxury but call for equally impressive furniture, pictures, carpets and furnishing fabrics to complement them.

In textiles, damask patterns are created by varying the direction of threads in a single-colour weave; in paper the contrasting pattern areas can be imitated by printing matt motifs onto a smooth, polished ground. Where the colour tone is identical or very similar, the effect closely resembles the fabrics that inspired these wallpapers. This plays tricks with the eye: sometimes you see the background shapes as dominant, sometimes the pattern catches the eye. Often, however, two distinct or contrasting colours are used, which throws the pattern more clearly into relief. Although the elaborate designs often echo those of flock papers, the smooth surface of damasks makes the overall effect somewhat lighter.

Walls hung with real damask or flock were beyond the means of the seventeenth-century English diarist Samuel Pepys who records that his wife's closet was done up in 'counterfeit damask'. Pepys would have wanted to emulate the rich hangings he admired in ceremonial state apartments and wealthy courtiers' rooms which he encountered in the course of his work as Chief Secretary to the Navy. The new damask effect paper was an affordable and stylish substitute which greatly appealed to the rising professional class of the time.

Traditional damask patterns are often not only intricate in outline but large in scale. It is normal to see such papers decorating large spaces such as the drawing rooms of great country houses or hotel ballrooms. But scale alone should not preclude using revivals of these papers in more modern surroundings; the recoloured versions of traditional designs could easily work in a contemporary setting. The designs are well balanced, with a harmonious relationship of pattern to background, and it is the very satisfactory evenness of this effect that can make damask designs work on a large scale without overwhelming a small room. Try the tactic of hanging a single roll of a design you like in a corner of the room: you may be surprised how a pattern which looked intimidating in the sample book suddenly comes to life on the wall, fitting in well with its scale and dimensions.

Moiré papers exploit the same principle of subtly contrasting matt and shiny areas of patterning, in this case in imitation of the magical effects played by light on the natural iridescence of silk that has been 'watermarked', that is, treated by intense pressure, heat and water or steam. Moiré papers contribute a beautifully quiet background, but with far more life than a flat painted wall. Traditional moiré texturing sometimes provided the ground for a printed motif, and sometimes ran in ribbon-like bands between other stripe effects.

Wallpaper manufacturers now make completely different styles of moiré, ranging from small unobtrusive patterns where, from a distance, all you notice is a slight movement of colour, to much bolder designs where the contrast of light and shade is more positively marked. Like large-scale damask designs these grander moiré patterns are very difficult to judge close to. The pattern may seem random and abstract as a small sample, but once on a wall its rhythm is revealed and the magnificent silken effect achieved.

FLORAL & FIGURATIVE PRINTED FABRICS

The fine patterns of printed fabrics have been another source of inspiration for wallpaper manufacturers. The two industries have often had much in common, although calico printers developed efficient machine-printing some half-century before wallpaper makers succeeded in mechanizing their process. Sometimes an attractive fabric print was taken and adapted for wallpaper, and an element of trompe l'oeil trickery lay behind some adoption of fabric patterns for papers. But probably just as important was the simple cross-fertilization of ideas from one material to another.

An early influence on wallpaper designs came from the bright colours and exotic patterns of the chintzes imported by the trading companies from India, some of which were used as wallhangings. British and French imitations were soon being produced in wallpapers as well as fabrics. By the end of the eighteenth century an increasingly large proportion of European wallpaper production featured the floral and figurative designs that have remained part of the tradition ever since. Manufacturers, particularly in France, had developed the skills and artistry to create fresh, lively motifs instead of the heavier formality of many earlier designs. The freer style owed a good deal to the influence of Oriental designs, and to the use of large woodblocks which allowed large-scale repeats and overall continuity.

Toile de Jouy paper designs were originally inspired by the manufacture of printed fabric at Jouy-en-Josas, a little village outside Paris, in the eighteenth century. Here the fabrics were printed on a

LEFT *The subtle vitality of a moiré paper brings the walls of an elegant London drawing room to life in a way that flat paint could never achieve. The full potential of moiré designs is often not realized until an expanse of paper is seen on the wall. It is hard to believe that this sophisticated effect is created by the same paper as the sample marked with stark white lines in the centre of the picture on page 16.*

BELOW *A strongly patterned toile de Jouy wallpaper is coordinated with a matching fabric covering the bed and chairs in this attic bedroom in Ireland.*

ABOVE *The traditional motifs of fabric design are adopted in this wallpaper which, with its light background and delicate colouring, gives the impression of a beautiful chintz.*

People often hesitate to spend as much on wallpaper as on fabric, fearing that it will not last – but the finest papers can give pleasure for decades. This lovely paper in a farmhouse hallway still looks superb after twenty years; many of the historic papers illustrated in this book have been in place for over a century.

RIGHT *Traditionally depicted in tones of rusty red, the finely drawn motifs in toile de Jouy fabrics print crisply on paper. Manufacturers sometimes produce the same pattern in both materials, presenting an ideal opportunity to create an integrated design scheme.*

neutral background, usually in red but sometimes in blue, brown or magenta. What made these so special was the combination of subject matter and printing technique: at the time it was an astonishing innovation to print fabric using an engraved copper roller. The result was like making prints, but using fabric instead of paper to print on: the technique allowed the engraver to adapt a huge variety of pictorial sources for fabric. One characteristic of toile de Jouy designs is the narrative element: some of them show jolly shepherds and shepherdesses in pastoral pleasures; others take scenes from classical mythology. Motifs from everyday life are another source and the strong influence of *Chinoiserie* is frequently seen. In English toile the subject matter was usually simpler, and both fabric and wallpaper reinterpretations show lively representations of trailing leaves, branches, birds, flowers and figures, all printed in line in a single colour.

These designs are ideal for coordinated fabric and paper effects, as their single-colour printing and natural background means that they can be used extensively without causing visual indigestion. They make a harmonious and delicate decoration very much in the French style. Other similar designs in single colours can also be chosen, but the finely etched lines of authentic Jouy papers give differing depths of tone and therefore more variety and life to the paper.

Other wallpapers printed to match fabric designs are widely available, but often come in several colours rather than the monotone effect of toile. Chintz patterns, especially, have inspired whole ranges of wallpapers and matching fabrics. Too much of too fussy a design can be excessive, and a wise course is to choose a combination of papers, fabrics and borders produced in coordinating colours but different patterns: many manufacturers group everything together making selection easier for you.

There is nothing new in this. There was a vogue for matching wallpapers and furnishing fabrics in the early eighteenth century; indeed, wallpaper makers were often involved in all aspects of interior design, choosing the fabrics for curtains and upholstery as well as supervising the decoration as a whole. Arts and Crafts and other late-nineteenth-century designers made fabrics and wallpapers to the same patterns, and a hundred years later the same idea lies behind the coordinated ranges of today.

DECORATIVE DRAPERY

Trompe l'oeil detailing featuring silky-textured fabrics twisted, draped, swagged, trimmed and tied into bows was a popular wallpaper theme in the early nineteenth century. Such effects naturally appeared as part of the elaborate floral designs produced by many French manufacturers, but in the form of borders and separate ornaments, fabric assumed a finishing role in room decoration which is enjoying a resurgence of popularity today.

French wallpapers depicted realistic-looking examples of the elaborate drapery styles in vogue. Some, for instance, represented life-sized satin curtains with highlights and shading very skilfully creating the illusion of pleats and folds. They were often trimmed with cords, tassels

and the elaborate passementerie of Empire ornamentation. Others were extravagant creations in lace, luxuriantly draped and finished with little flourishes of frills and scalloped edges. Posies of flowers were added at intervals and just for good measure a few ribbons and bows kept the whole design together.

There are document reproductions of these opulent French lacy designs, and in the right location they can look delightful. Lace wallpaper is so pretty when seen in small pieces that it is easy to fall in love with the idea and fail to visualize its impact *en masse*. Unless the rest of the decoration is suitably restrained, the result can look completely over the top. Waking up in a bedroom with lace all over the walls is like finding yourself in the middle of a soufflé.

Easier to use are the simpler versions of trompe l'oeil lace wallpaper, re-created from the very earliest examples, which perfectly capture the lightness and delicacy of lace. The design is printed in white over a coloured ground, so that different tones are created according to the closeness of the pattern. Quite another impression is given when the printing is reversed and a dark pattern is printed on a light background: it looks less like lace, and the overall rhythm of the pattern is predominant.

The intricate patterns of lace and embroideries have inspired designs for wallpaper from its earliest days.

This delicate wallpaper (ABOVE) resembling draped bridal lace takes its inspiration from a French design of the nineteenth century.

Papers inspired by lace (LEFT) can be dramatic as well as refined. The paper on the floor is a copy of a seventeenth-century design and bears a strong resemblance to the fine blackwork embroideries of the period.

FAR LEFT *Wallpaper printed to look like silk drapery creates an astonishing effect in this hallway, its opulence being entirely in keeping with the neo-classical architecture. The folds of fabric seem to be held up by the cornice and drape in sumptuous swathes towards the floor.*

ELEMENTS OF ARCHITECTURE

Trompe l'oeil paper effects imitating structural elements of interiors such as pillars, dados and cornices have long been popular among designers for their ability to adjust the apparent proportions of rooms according to favoured principles and to provide just the right finishing framework to more fanciful pictorial and other decorative papers.

In some periods and styles only selected elements are deemed appropriate, like the balustrading effects applied to the dado section of walls adorned with scenic wallpapers, or the deep plasterwork-effect friezes and coffered ceiling designs that became popular in the late nineteenth century.

In periods when neo-classicism has exercised a strong influence, the entire vocabulary of classical ornament has been called into play, with three-dimensional niches and statuary providing focal points on walls enlivened with the illusion of horizontal divisions and vertical columns. Decorating an interior with these elements was a serious business, for the paperhanger had to deploy the relief-effect mouldings and other elements in correct relation to the room's main source of light as well as conforming to strict principles of order and proportion.

The flourish of decorative plasterwork has frequently been imitated in wallpaper. Elaborate Rococo mouldings and *Chinoiserie*-inspired motifs can be seen in historic papers – the scrolls and cartouches formed by the fake plaster often containing little scenes or vignettes like the print room paper on page 140. Some designs are more classical in appearance, perhaps reflecting the influence of the superb plaster decoration in the interiors designed by Robert Adam. In Edwardian England delicate papers in plain colours were enlivened with elegant arabesques, urns and ribbons with highly convincing trompe l'oeil plasterwork.

Certain specialist companies still print a repertoire of separate architectural elements such as borders and mouldings, as well as more elaborate motifs such as pilasters and columns, for enterprising decorators to incorporate into room schemes. They range in style from the classical to reinterpretations of the Gothick style.

FINE BUILDING MATERIALS

Fake marbling has been a stock in trade of the painter's craft for centuries, transforming wood and plasterwork to create the illusion of the more expensive material. Wallpapers, too, have been made to resemble various kinds of marble, as well as other masonry, with equal conviction. In the last century, stone and marble effects were deemed particularly suitable for hallways, sometimes accompanied by ornate trompe l'oeil architectural elements.

The natural colouring of stone wallpaper is a surprisingly effective background for pictures and its simplicity makes it a perfect foil for furniture. With its clean-cut style it can look particularly good in many present-day entrance halls – in spite of their being considerably less grand than the stone-clad castle walls that inspired the paper. The wall-like illusion of blocks of stone is sometimes quite simply achieved by a grid of pale lines representing mortar. Other papers are more three-dimensional and look like great wedges of smooth hewn stone or ashlar.

LEFT *A small room in this villa in Tuscany is hung with a magnificent eighteenth-century French wallpaper. The three-dimensional effect of the columns and arches is achieved by the contrast of light and shade.*

BELOW *This modern interpretation of an eighteenth-century theme explores the Gothic vocabulary of architectural ornament rather than the classical. The eye is drawn into a landscape of trompe l'oeil fantasy with imaginary follies and castle ruins.*

LEFT *The three-dimensional appearance of these friezes and borders creates the effect of intricate plaster moulding. Even such small amounts of plaster detailing can set a style for the entire room, and the pointed arches, quatrefoils and rosettes here combine to achieve a delightful echo of eighteenth-century Gothick. This light and delicate style came to be spelled with a final 'k' to distinguish it from the medieval Gothic which inspired it and from the later Victorian revival.*

The impression can be completed with stone flags or tiles on the floor.

Among the most popular *faux* effects in wallpaper today are the papers printed in imitation of marble. At their simplest, marble effects may be little more than an expanse of flat colour broken with just enough light veining to give life to the surface. Really expensive hand-painted marble papers are obviously the most lustrous and convincing because the veining evolves over the paper in exactly the same way as in genuine marble; there is no obvious repeat. However, marble-effect paper is best in smaller areas rather than wall-to-wall – not only because large expanses can evoke the spartan atmosphere of a health club, but because this is not the way real marble is usually seen.

It is much more exciting to reinterpret traditional marble decoration in contrasting borders and panels (see pages 102–103). Marble occurs naturally in an enormous variety of colours, but you can also find *faux* marble papers tinted turquoise or other completely artificial colours. It is best to stick to the natural warm tones of Italian marble – rose pink, sienna yellow, ochre, flame, rich dark greens, mellow browns, black veined with grey, grey veined with white, white with grey veining, and

RIGHT *Stone provides a magnificently weighty subject for wallpaper designs. The effect they achieve is usually determined by the treatment of the joins between the blocks. If they look deeply recessed and moulded by light and shade, as in the paper on the rear wall, the effect is massive. When the mortar is indicated by nothing more than a simple line, however, as in the papers on the ground and the one hanging on the left of the picture, they are far more restrained in their impact.*

every conceivable variation on the same theme. You can also consider combining some of the more realistic stone-effect papers such as the speckled greys of granite with the rich penetrating blue of lapis lazuli or the vivid green gradations of malachite, all of which contrast superbly with the restrained coolness of marbled papers.

Like marbling, fake wood-graining has an honourable pedigree: for centuries people have sought to upgrade the timber of their buildings and furniture to make it resemble the fashionable wood of the moment – oak, mahogany, rosewood, even bamboo. In the eighteenth and nineteenth centuries wood-effect wallpaper designs, combed by hand or block-printed, imitated wainscoting and carved wood panelling. They were often intended for dados, and, as with other architectural papers, were much advocated for hallways. Using different panels it was possible to build up quite complex arrangements of dados, cornices, pillars and panelling in between. Trompe l'oeil techniques could create the illusion of relief carvings and mouldings. Some French nineteenth-century papers were designed to frame scenic papers with the effect of wooden architectural elements, allowing the landscape in the panorama to dissolve into the distance. Popular in Germany at the same time were wallpapers which imitated a kind of 'hunting lodge' decorative style, depicting dark wood with heavily carved columns and niches – some with carved trophies of dead game arranged within them.

A number of traditional designs are still in production today, and panelled papers with dados, or even dados themselves, can bring a touch

ABOVE *The subtle colours and rich veining of natural marble provide the inspiration for this wallpaper. With its warm tones and fine texturing it has a greater flexibility than some of the more grandiose marble-effect designs. It can look as much at home in unpretentious cottage settings as in more sophisticated interiors.*

LEFT *A collection of wood papers that not only look convincingly like different timbers but also have the pleasing tactile quality of wood's natural grain.*

FAR LEFT *A crisply defined stone-effect wallpaper produces a cool dignified effect in this dining area. Natural light filtering through the blind, rather than ornament and pattern, provides the decoration (see also page 156).*

The idea of trellis usually conjures an image of a wooden lattice for training plants in the garden. Indeed, many wallpapers have been based on this, sometimes printed just as plain trellis and sometimes festooned with flowers and leaves. Stone can also be used to create an intricate trellis and this paper richly illustrates a Gothic stone effect. The coloured ground seems to represent the surface of the wall while the carved stone lacework appears to stand out in three-dimensional relief.

of grandeur in the appropriate setting. Modern wood-effect papers are far less ornate and fit easily into contemporary settings. Some simply resemble planks – not necessarily the ubiquitous pine 'tongue and groove', but wider boards with an interesting grain and realistic-looking raised finish. Pale colours grained with grey reminiscent of driftwood give a pretty light panelled effect; mellower tones with the warmth of natural wood bring a 'back to the country' feel.

TRELLISWORK

Wallpapers imitating trellis appear to pierce the wall's surface, taking the eye through to an apparent space behind the grid of bamboo, stone, fretwork or garden trellis and so creating a delightful airy feeling. Stone-effect trellis looks almost like the icing on a wedding-cake and creates a light and delicate atmosphere. Green trellis, or a fretwork that looks like wood, can bring a fresh, conservatory-like atmosphere to lighten a dark room, particularly when partnered with foliage and flower borders.

Many trellis designs have traditionally been used as dado papers, and this provides an opportunity for combining two patterned papers without their designs overpowering each other. A bamboo trellis or a fretwork design will complement Chinese-style papers particularly well and build up a distinctive theme for a room. A quite different mood is achieved by using a garden trellis paper as a dado with a lively floral paper above.

Trellis is also the inspiration for hundreds of geometric wallpapers, designed as flat patterns without the three-dimensional element and varying in size from the tiniest diamonds which hardly register as pattern when seen from a distance to large, bold outlines. While these patterns can look simple and attractive in the small swatch in a pattern book, once seen on the wall, the geometry may take on another character, and form completely different shapes, perhaps moving in long intersecting diagonal lines or enclosing the room in a cagelike grid. It may be wise to ask for a large sample before making a purchase.

PAINT EFFECTS & STENCILLING

The time-honoured distressed paint finishes that have recently been revived as decorating fashions have been perfectly imitated in wallpaper. Wallpaper versions of dragging and ragging, splattering and sponging and many other processes with vigorous-sounding names all make pleasant, subtly textured wall surfaces without the anxiety and effort of Doing It Yourself with messy paint, pigment and glaze.

Stencilling, another traditional form of wall decoration based on paint, has influenced wallpaper designs in a number of ways, both in the types of pattern produced and in the textural quality of the painted colour. Indeed, when the earliest wallpapers were printed only in black, stencilling was one way of adding any additional colours required. The result was a rather blotchy, inaccurate effect, similar to the paper lining the chest on page 150, with an element of unsophisticated charm that later eyes have found attractive.

Many of the wallpaper and border designs of the pre-First World War era were based on stencilling with their pools of bright jewel-like colours shading gently inside thickly drawn black outlining. Other designs are built up without the outlining, with colours softly fusing across the paper. William Shand Kydd's spectacular wide friezes in this style made a dramatic design statement around a room, with bold motifs filling large lengths of wall space (see page 86).

Skilled artists and craftsmen are producing hand-stencilled wallpaper today, but since the method is so time-consuming, the results are expensive. Stencilling also offers a way of patterning your own paper, starting on wallpaper printed with a plain background colour, or using lining paper and colouring your own ground. You can work directly on the wall if you are doing it in your own home; only if you are producing the paper for someone else does it make sense to stencil the paper before hanging it.

Some of the prettiest designs available now are the simplest repeated patterns, running like stripes up the wall. This is most likely a hark-back to hand-stencilling on wooden walls, when the painted planks would have formed a ready-made framework of wide vertical bands. Decorating the walls with stencilled motifs was popular in rural communities in Scandinavia and in eighteenth-century America, when it was difficult to obtain wallpaper, and the charming patterns from these sources provide perennial inspiration for subsequent designers. With the revival of interest in simple, country styles of decoration, stencilled and stencil-effect papers, which are both charming and easy to live with, have enjoyed a renewed vogue.

BELOW LEFT *Many popular paint effects are easily and expertly imitated by wallpapers, which display an evenness of design and lightness of texture that non-professionals find hard to perfect in paint. This stippled paper provides a simple but attractively broken textured background for the unassuming furniture and pictures in a Swedish country cottage.*

BELOW RIGHT *The effect of stencilling is to create flat areas of colour with softly blurred edges (see also page 86). This small Gothick study is hung with a hand-printed wallpaper. The colour is applied so lightly in some areas that a variation in depth is achieved, convincingly reproducing the effect of hand-stencilling.*

PICTORIAL EFFECTS

*I*t is possible to trace the pedigree of pictorial wall decoration back to the murals of Knossos, Pompeii and Herculaneum, with antecedents in Egyptian tomb decoration and prehistoric cave paintings at Lascaux. But it was the church frescoes of medieval Italy which led to the great secular flowering of mural painting during the Renaissance when this form of decorative art reached its zenith. Artists skilled in the use of perspective depicted colourful, dramatic scenes with intense realism on palazzo walls. In addition to these pictorial skills, painters developed techniques of light-and-shade that exploited eye-deceiving three-dimensional effects, so that architectural ornament such as painted scrollwork, trophies and other devices could be made to seem to stand out in relief. This illusionist vision – as opposed to abstract, two-dimensional pattern-making – has been one of the major influences on design since wallpapers were first printed.

Painterly effects in wallpapers embrace both 'pictures' – scenes such as landscapes and panoramas – and some of the more stylized patterns in which elements such as foliage and draperies are treated in a three-dimensional way.

Some very rich and rare wallpapers are actually hand-painted, not printed: antique Chinese papers depicting birds and flowers are examples, in a tradition that continues today. Many more wallpapers are produced which replicate the effects of hand-painting. For more than two centuries manufacturers have gone to great lengths to try to reproduce the impression of artists' brushstrokes and gradations of colour by mechanical means. Modern manufacturing methods can produce impressions as light and translucent as watercolour, but more traditional printing methods rely on many different colours to build up a hand-painted look.

CHINESE WALLPAPERS

Some of the most beautiful and desirable wallpapers ever produced are the exquisite hand-painted papers from China. Produced in sets, they are designed to make a continuous display around the room, each panel linking with the next. The earliest designs feature birds and flowers with foliage, painted on a background of plain colour, often pale blue, grey, cream or light green. The design is light and free and the drawing is in outline filled with clear bright colours. Branches of bamboo and flowering shrubs intermingle, while peonies and roses flower amidst waving grass. Birds, butterflies and other insects, painted with extraordinary botanical accuracy, fly, strut and perch among the leaves. A trellis or fence may be added at the bottom of some papers, changing

Chinese hand-painted panoramas are designed to form a continuous decoration round the room. In the eighteenth century some featured flowers and flowing branches decorated with exotic birds while others, such as this one, were more complex narrative compositions. They showed large numbers of people engrossed in daily activities, from silk weaving to growing tea, and provide fascinating insights into life in China at the time. Here people are shown arriving at a tea house for the social ceremony that was an important aspect of civilized Chinese life.

Chinese papers can transform a room totally, creating a unique sense of depth and space, despite the absence of perspective in the western sense.

This detail comes from the wallpaper hung in the boardroom of Coutts Bank in London. Lord Macartney, who was Britain's first ambassador to China, gave the paper to the founder of the bank, Thomas Coutts, in 1794.

The Chinese dressing room is one of four rooms at Saltram House in Devon in which Chinese papers survive.

This type of paper was often known as India paper in the eighteenth century because it was shipped to England by the East India Company.

angles as it winds around the room and giving the design a base.

Papers introduced after about 1750 became more complicated. They are narrative in composition, showing large numbers of people engaged in trading or daily activities such as farming, hunting or making porcelain. Tea production was a frequent theme and workers are shown busily planting, harvesting, drying, packing, and selling the tea.

When traders first began to bring Chinese wallpaper back to Europe at the end of the seventeenth century, the idea of hanging paper on the walls was already established but the sheer quality and originality of the Chinese imports easily surpassed anything else available. Soon the owners of great houses were clamouring for a Chinese room, hung with Chinese wallpaper, as a suitable background to a collection of Chinese lacquer furniture, vases and ornaments. Since the paper was so expensive it was only hung in important rooms, usually a principal bedroom.

During the eighteenth century the fashion spread throughout Europe as well as to America, and rooms with beautiful original Chinese wallpaper that is still intact can be seen in stately homes and old Colonial houses today. At Temple Newsam, near Leeds in West Yorkshire, the Chinese wallpaper was hung as late as the 1820s, when the fashion was

LEFT *A dressing room in the theatre at Drottningholm Castle in Sweden is decorated in the* Chinoiserie *style. The individual panels in original Chinese panoramas unfold in a non-repeating scene but here the same tree and bird design is repeated on each panel, suggesting that an eighteenth-century Swedish artist had been inspired by seeing a single drop of an imported Chinese paper.*

BELOW *Decorative birds and flowers typical of the earliest Chinese papers are combined with figures, characteristic of later designs.*

beginning to wane. Perhaps Lady Hertford, who had received the paper as a gift from her admirer the Prince of Wales some years before, was not given sufficient paper, or perhaps she favoured a more highly decorated room, but to cover up the blank spaces she carefully cut out extra birds from John James Audubon's recently published *The Birds of America* and pasted them up as required. Such a solution is hardly to be recommended with Audubon prints today, but it illustrates the way in which a certain amount of judicious cutting out and pasting was to be expected to ensure continuity and harmony in the arrangement of the panels, particularly in awkward places where doorways, windows and fireplaces break the expanse of wall. Indeed, both plain, undecorated rolls and pieces with extra painted birds, butterflies and so on were often supplied with the main panels.

It is not difficult to see why Chinese wallpapers have always been so highly prized. Quite apart from the fact that they are completely different from any other form of wallpaper, they are beautifully executed paintings which can completely transform a room.

It is possible to obtain historic Chinese papers today from certain specialist dealers – at unbelievable prices. An alternative at more accessible price levels is to look for the imported modern hand-painted Chinese papers, executed in the traditional way, or for the faithful reproductions of original designs which are made by specialist studios in the West. Even now a complete Chinese panorama can be created with all the charm of the original inspiration, but planning and hanging the wallpaper is complicated and should be done by a professional.

ABOVE *The passion for Chinese wallpaper was so widespread in the eighteenth century that many grand country houses had at least one room decorated in this way. This beautiful paper, with an unusual silvery white background, is in Burton Constable Hall near Hull.*

RIGHT *A modern, hand-painted Chinese wallpaper in an elegant London drawing room incorporates traditional elements of seventeenth-century paper – branches, flowers and exotic birds.*

THE INFLUENCE OF REVEILLON

Chinese wallpapers established a taste for beautiful hand-printed wallpapers and encouraged European makers, especially in France and England, to be more creative in their designs. One of the most famous was the French wallpaper maker Jean-Baptiste Réveillon, whose papers are still regarded as supreme examples of the art. For some years before the French Revolution his factory in Paris produced the finest and most beautiful wallpapers for the French aristocracy; when it was sacked by the angry mob in 1789, Réveillon fled to England. But his factory was reopened later by others who found favour with the Revolutionaries by printing patriotic papers in red, white and blue and were thereby enabled also to continue the production of earlier, more elegant designs.

Some of the most exquisite of Réveillon's papers took their inspiration directly from the painted decoration with which artists were embellishing wooden panelling, doors and shutters. Raphael had originated this style in his decoration of rooms in the Vatican Palace in Rome, but soon after it was being copied in palaces all over Europe. Réveillon successfully adapted the effect to wallpaper. Classically inspired, the papers feature long vertical designs of urns, flowers, curved-necked swans, birds and beasts in graceful arabesques, block-printed in dozens of different colours. The designs flow from a central

The front sitting room in the Phelps-Hatheway House in Connecticut was hung with a Réveillon-style wallpaper in 1795. The delicate arrangements of flower garlands, urns and arabesques on a light background are characteristic of Réveillon designs.

The paper is elegantly finished off by borders which pick out all the architectural features of the room – doors, dados, chimney breast. The horizontal borders, with pink roses, are wide; the vertical ones, with a geometric pattern, are narrow.

stem which evolves upwards, interrupted by plaques and roundels containing figure compositions. They were usually intended to be hung as panels, separated by borders and plain wallpaper sections.

Réveillon's artists also took much of their classical inspiration from the archeological excavations of the mid-eighteenth century, when the discovery of the Roman wall paintings of Pompeii and Herculaneum had considerable impact on contemporary taste. Having lain undisturbed since Vesuvius erupted in AD 79, the decorations, which mostly consisted of large panels with ornate borders, were wonderfully preserved. Strongly contrasting Mediterranean colours – glowing reds, ochres, terracottas, rich greens, azure blues – were used together with large areas of black. Classical motifs, medallions and dancing figures filled the panel area. All were adapted and imitated in the new classical-style wallpapers produced by Réveillon (see pages 6–7).

Their superb quality and artistry ensured Réveillon papers an appreciative market way beyond the shores of his native France. They were a very popular import in America during the eighteenth century and many can still be seen in New England houses.

Careful reproductions of Réveillon designs have been made by several eminent wallpaper manufacturers. More widely available are copies of papers in the Réveillon style. These are produced to run as continuous wall-to-wall decoration rather than in panels, but with imagination they can be adapted, as in the bedroom on page 101.

Réveillon's wallpapers have inspired many modern interpretations. The classical design (ABOVE RIGHT) was carefully copied from a paper hanging in the Phelps-Hatheway House. The paper next to it is also available today and is an interpretation of a design held in the manufacturer's archive.

French panoramic wallpapers introduced in the United States in the nineteenth century were received enthusiastically. They quickly became fashionable status symbols and enhanced the homes of many prosperous families, where they can often still be seen today.

This scenic panorama draws the viewer into an elegantly landscaped garden in France.

Such papers were never very popular in England – perhaps because the English were less attracted by this kind of visual trickery, perhaps because panoramas left little space to display the ancestral portraits with which they liked to surround themselves.

PANORAMIC LANDSCAPES

The Chinese concept of a continuous pictorial decoration covering all the walls of a room gave rise to European imitations, and some delightful pastiche designs. At the beginning of the nineteenth century a western successor to the Chinese panorama emerged, from European manufacturers who were now capable of producing wallpaper of high quality and considerable sophistication. As an astonishing decorative and technical achievement, the panoramic papers developed principally by the Zuber company of Rixheim and by Dufour in Mâcon and Paris have never been equalled.

A panoramic paper is like a continuous mural painting, but instead of being commissioned specially and painted *in situ* over months or years by an individual artist, these landscapes were block-printed by hand onto rolls of wallpaper. Never before had wallpaper printing been attempted on such a scale. In order to cover the walls of large rooms without repeating a scene, twenty or thirty lengths were printed; some panoramic sets required up to fifty. Each length was about 3 metres/10 feet high by 50 centimetres/20 inches wide. Printing them called for thousands of hand-carved blocks and hundreds of colours. Creating even one panorama meant an enormous investment of time and risk for

the manufacturers in what was a completely new concept in interior decoration. And yet their entrepreneurial daring paid off. The panoramas were an immediate success and found an enthusiastic market in France, Europe and the United States throughout the nineteenth century, though they were never popular in England.

The popularity of the papers lay not in the general admiration of the technical skill behind them, but in their unique ability to break through space. The viewer is no longer conscious of being confined within the walls of a room, but by a trick of the eye is apparently outdoors, surveying an infinitely distant horizon. The artists took care to alternate close-up detail, scenes in the middle distance and glimpses of the horizon

Exotic, far-off lands were popular subjects for panoramas. This panel is part of the French panorama 'Natives of the Pacific', 1804. It is based on the discoveries of the explorer and navigator Captain Cook in the South Seas.

Such graphic, though often fanciful, revelations of distant countries and foreign peoples must have had a dramatic impact.

to achieve their effects. Zuber were especially skilled at creating an illusion of ever-deepening space by their realistic printing of the sky. This was done before the woodblocks were used, and a technique was perfected to produce an even gradation of tones from the palest yellow or pink tinge on the horizon to a deeper blue at the top of the panel.

Scenic themes were also popular because they transported viewers to exotic locations far away from everyday life. The city dweller could find escape in far-off lands, both real and imagined: he could surround himself with picturesque Alpine scenery or share the discoveries of Captain Cook in the South Pacific. Trade between France and North America flourished and scenic papers purchased then are still to be seen in Colonial houses in the United States; New Englanders were intrigued with topographical views of distant Europe or proudly surrounded themselves with the spectacular 'Views of North America' produced in 1834. In 1852 Zuber took advantage of a wave of nationalist feeling in the American market and republished this paper as 'The War of American Independence', substituting the foreground figures so that Boston Harbour became the scene of the Boston Tea Party and once-peaceful landscapes turned into battle-sites full of soldiers and smoke. Precise authenticity was not demanded or expected in scenic wallpapers.

Classical mythology provided another rich source of subjects, and these panoramas were often printed in grisaille, imitating reliefs in various shades of grey, a technique perfected by Dufour (see page 69). These gradations of colour naturally required far fewer blocks to achieve their sculptural effect than did full-colour panoramas, but their understated quality has its own particular beauty.

Zuber, the same company who produced the great scenic panoramas of the nineteenth century, are today re-creating some of them for modern use. Other companies produce designs based on similar themes intended to convert into a continuous scene, also printed by hand, but a taste for panoramic decoration is still expensive to indulge.

LEFT *Thirty-three drops of wallpaper, each with a different scene designed to link with the next, make up the complete panorama 'Vues d'Italie' designed for Zuber in France in 1823. In this drawing room it is hung in separate panels.*

It is printed in grisaille, the various shades of grey creating a convincing impression of depth and perspective.

BELOW *To help potential purchasers envisage the final effect, samples showed complete panoramas on a much-reduced scale. It was not necessary to order the whole run, and careful planning was needed to decide on the number of drops required and the best way to arrange them. These samples show 'Views of North America', at the top and below it, 'Hindustan', the modern reprint of which is illustrated overleaf.*

A modern reprint of the spectacular 'Hindustan' panorama hangs in a London dining room. Over one thousand different blocks and eighty-five different colours were used to print the original, with its twenty panels designed to hang in a continuous sequence.

Pierre-Antoine Mongin designed 'Hindustan' for the Zuber company in 1807. He used as reference the carefully observed watercolours and drawings of Thomas and William Daniell who had recently travelled in India. Nonetheless, alongside the fairly accurate portrayals of palaces, tombs and temples, his work incorporates some charming elements of fantasy.

The detail (ABOVE) shows a panel from the same panorama.

REPEAT PATTERN

O f all the different wallpaper styles a flat repeating pattern printed on paper designed to hang from wall to ceiling, wall to wall, is the image which occurs to most people when wallpaper is mentioned. Easily the largest volume of wallpapers produced fall into this category. The underlying principle of all patterns is to make an overall decoration with an unobtrusively repeating motif, but the result is an enormous variety of different effects. The elements may be small and subtle, bold and eye-catching – or anything in between. The pattern may 'read' from a distance as a series of regularly spaced dots or motifs, a diagonally based diaper arrangement, an all-over floral motif, a stripe or a continuous interweaving effect. Pronounced colour contrasts will make the elements stand out; close gradations of colour or tone give a gentler impact.

Many of the patterns available to us today are authentic reproductions of old designs, often copied from small fragments found in old houses. But often designs and motifs are reproduced – or adapted and reinterpreted – without particular reference to their earlier incarnation, and when you choose a wallpaper from a pattern book you do not necessarily know its antecedents. Much of the 'vocabulary' of pattern is very ancient, emerging again and again in new guises. And every so often a new 'language' of pattern emerges, such as the highly articulated appreciation of flat, two-dimensional design that emerged in English wallpapers of the second half of the last century.

STRIPED WALLPAPERS

Stripes are a special sort of flat pattern. Striped designs have a most remarkable versatility and can add a striking elegance to a wide variety of settings. A stripe can vary in width and effect from the muted displacement of colour of dragged paintwork or a close arrangement of matt and shiny textures, to very broad vertical bands which are visually arresting wherever they are hung. Plain stripes can alternate with a pattern – an abstract, floral or geometric design in between each straight band adds an extra dimension and breaks the rigid symmetry of a conventional hard-edged stripe. A stripe can fill the entire width of the wallpaper, with just a slim border design running down one side. This hardly looks like a stripe in the sample book, but hung on the wall at once reveals its pronounced vertical divisions.

The character of a striped wallpaper and its decorative effect is decided much more by the combination of colours than in the arrangement or width of the stripes. A pale colour, alternating with white, will have a fresh, sunny informal look, which looks attractive with light wood, cane, or painted pieces of furniture. A mixture of strong, deep colours will produce a richer, more sophisticated effect and is a wonderful background for mahogany and oak. A closely toned combination of

The 'Gothic Lily' pattern is one of several wallpapers designed in the 1840s by A.W.N. Pugin for the Palace of Westminster. Pugin, a distinguished Victorian architect and designer, was passionately interested in medieval style and among the leaders of the wave of interest in the Gothic Revival.

Bold repeating patterns printed in vibrantly strong colours are the hallmark of his wallpapers. Here interlinking strapwork weaves around stylized Tudor roses and lilies on a background of rich forest green which throws the design into prominence.

This paper can be printed today using the original blocks in any combination of colours (see page 8).

stripes provides an excellent background for pictures and furniture, while strongly contrasting stripes make such an impact they may detract from, rather than enhance, objects displayed against them.

Stripes are one kind of wallpaper in which hand-printing does not promise a superior product. Neither the woodblock technique nor screen-printing are particularly suitable for producing long straight lines, because every time the block or screen is printed there is a chance of misalignment and a consequent wobble where the lines join. Before the invention of mechanical production methods they were made with a long 'v'-shaped trough which was divided into sections with slots at the base. The paint was poured into the trough and the paper pulled through at speed underneath. Modern manufacturing techniques are a distinct improvement. Also, since the design element in a stripe is so basic, very inexpensive papers can look just as effective as expensive ones – there is no need for extravagance in making an attractive decoration, although some ranges may have more subtlety and variety in their colourings.

Stripes have the great advantage of being relatively timeless, which means that the decoration will not date, unlike some designs which can look very *passé* after a few years. Nor do stripes impose a particular style

Green and buff stripes are enlivened by the addition of a richly textured floral pattern. The colours are echoed in the brightly painted door and dado, lending an air of cheerful informality to this period bedroom.

on a room, demanding, for instance, a country living feel with rustic pine or a collection of precious antique furniture.

Many of the more decorative striped patterns were originally copied from textiles and the combination of the stripe interspersed with other patterns like flowers produces a much softer feel – more akin to fabric. Some moirés are produced as stripes giving a combination of sheen and matt in the most understated patterns. Some reproduce the effect of checked taffeta or watered silk stripes. Most up to date are the wallpaper designs taken from ethnic woven fabrics – Indian Ikat designs and richly coloured stripes from Asia and North Africa. Hung on the walls and taken up over the ceiling, they can create the effect of a sumptuously hung bedouin tent.

Striped rooms with the wallpaper continued on to the ceiling (see page 114) were popular in Regency England and Napoleonic France; indeed, the fashion cropped up all over Europe. The effect was of a campaign tent, where everything, including the furniture, had to be instantly transportable. It was an example of current events – the Napoleonic wars – affecting contemporary taste. Rooms like this are easy to copy using striped papers in brisk military colours – rich reds, Prussian blues, dark greens or greys – and finishing them off with rope borders to add to the illusion. The furniture can be chosen to complement the style – plain dark furniture, imposing lamps, antique rugs on the wooden floor and curtains hung from poles with arrow-heads and quivers as finials, in true Napoleonic style.

The fashion for stripes in the Regency gave its name to the idea of Regency Stripe and rooms decorated in this way take on an air of elegant formality. Hallways are particularly suited to striped wallpaper either from wall to ceiling, or contrasting with a plain dado. In any room where the feeling of height needs to be increased, stripes will help visually to heighten the ceiling.

ABOVE LEFT *Elegant and plain, an even stripe in taupe and cream provides the perfect foil to this carefully balanced arrangement of objects and furniture. Its clean lines echo the classical austerity of the magnificent marble floor, while the warmer colours offset the coolness of the stone.*

ABOVE RIGHT *An Empire stripe with different widths and colours brings a variety of surface pattern and an element of vitality to the walls.*

ABOVE *A flowing design of tulips and butterflies adapted for wallpaper from an original chintz pattern.*

RIGHT *Ribbon interweaving through stylized leaves and flowers brings movement to this bold repeat pattern. It makes an emphatic statement in this entrance hall and shows how large dramatic patterns can work effectively in a small space.*

ALL-OVER PATTERN

The origins of repeating wallpaper patterns go back to the earliest papers for walls, printed in small pieces, when the blocks used to print them simply stamped the same design on each piece. Later on when wallpapers came to be produced mechanically on a roller the same constraints applied, with the design repeating as the roller revolved. Many patterns consist of isolated motifs arranged on a ground, but in others the shapes or lines continue across the paper joining each length to the next. Considerable skill has been exercised by designers to ensure that these patterns flow uninterruptedly; it has even sometimes been a tenet of design that repeats should be not merely unobtrusive but virtually invisible.

Mass production has given wallpaper patterns a bad press, aggravated by contrasting their repetitive quality with the relatively lively and glamorous character of the hand-printed panoramas and specialized three-dimensional effects. But good all-over patterns have a strength and logic of their own, and their abstract qualities are a complete contrast to figurative designs.

In mid-nineteenth-century England many of the finest wallpaper designers worked quite consciously to refine patterns that were unashamedly two-dimensional. They were reacting against both the excesses of many of the exuberant three-dimensional designs then favoured in France, and to the inferior imitations produced in England and America, which lacked the skill and panache of the originals, as well as to the mindless, over-ornate patternmaking that the newly mechanized wallpaper industry was providing for a growing domestic market.

LEFT *Wallpapers are not constrained by nature, and blue fuchsias make an attractive pattern. These leafy sprays flow freely across walls and ceiling with almost imperceptible repeats and unnoticeable joins in the best traditions of all-over design. The pale background and delicate figuring of this paper and the matching fabric retain the room's light, airy feel while achieving a coordinated finish.*

BELOW *'Berkeley Sprig', a simple repeating bell-flower motif on a diaper ground, suggests the stitched look of antique quilts. This paper was copied from a fragment found during the renovation of an eighteenth-century house in Berkeley Square, London.*

The plea went up to use decoration honestly to make walls intrinsically beautiful as walls, and not to pretend that they were landscapes, that plants appeared to be twining up them or niches and pillars breaking their surface. Critics and designers became positively puritanical in their condemnation of what they saw as fakery and illusion.

The movement was heralded by a revival of interest in the Gothic style of decoration led by the architect and designer A.W.N. Pugin. He was responsible for the medieval-inspired wallpapers for the Palace of Westminster in the late 1840s, and developed designs of strong repeating motifs and stylized flowers. Pugin's magnificent papers are still produced today from the original blocks, but need suitably baronial interiors to look their best; more restrained reinterpretations are also available for people who like the style but are daunted by the sheer scale or the very dominant quality of the original colours (see pages 8 and 47).

Pugin's dislike of three-dimensional tricks was shared by the eminent designer Owen Jones. His book *The Grammar of Ornament*, published in 1856, exerted a strong influence on every aspect of decorative art. It brought public attention to the need for high standards in design, to prevent what Jones saw as the continuous debasement of public taste.

THE INFLUENCE OF WILLIAM MORRIS

In agreement with Jones, William Morris pursued the same theme. His wallpaper designs present a softer and slightly less formalized interpretation of the credo that wallpaper pattern should be 'honest', incorporating no tricks designed to deceive the eye. Instead of the rather static emblematic motifs of the Gothic-style patterns, Morris's wallpapers

ABOVE *William Morris's 'Bower' wallpaper, first produced in 1877, demonstrates his superb handling of complex repeating patterns. Light and dark areas and large and small floral motifs are balanced in a lively overall decoration which intrigues the eye without resolving into any unintended shapes or distracting directional lines.*

RIGHT *In the Acanthus Room at Wightwick Manor, built in the late 1880s and decorated in the Arts and Crafts taste, the original Morris wallpaper shows a confident use of large-scale design in a relatively small space. The twelve-block pattern of swirling leaves is taken past the picture rail to ceiling height. In the green-painted area behind the pictures the wallpaper was removed following water damage.*

have a strongly organic quality. He followed the dictum that forms should be abstracted from nature and stylized, not imitative. His plants are recognizable and graceful; though painted in areas of flat colour, often with firm outlining, the flowers flow and curve across the paper. There is no modelling in darker and lighter tones, but a feeling of depth is created by shading in strong stylized lines. His leaves and stems intertwine as if in a lightly blowing breeze, their natural forms flowing freely in spite of being rendered in only two dimensions. Above all, he used the idea of the repeat in a masterly way, demonstrating his ability 'to mask the construction of our pattern enough to prevent people from counting repeats'.

The effect of William Morris and his fellow-members of the Arts and Crafts Movement – and subsequent followers, such as C.F.A. Voysey – has been incalculable, changing peoples' ideas of decoration first in England and then the United States. Morris's name is a household word in a way few designers have ever achieved. His patterns are still popular, not just for wallpapers and fabrics, but scaled down and adapted to all sorts of domestic items.

The concept underpinning Morris's designs – that of two-dimensional flat pattern repeating as the block-printing process allows – worked superbly for him but, once exposed to a mechanized manufacturing process it has, in lesser hands, led to thousands of unimaginative and repetitious wallpapers. Morris wanted to make available the best in craftsmanship and design to a wider range of society. The manufacturing process itself has indeed enabled the price of printing wallpaper to tumble, making it a commodity affordable to everyone, but the quality of design in the cheapest papers is often depressingly dull. This may explain why reproductions of 'classic' patterns, particularly small decorative motifs and floral designs, are so popular. This is not simply part of a fashion for the antique, but a recognition of the enduring quality of these traditional designs.

Laura Ashley captured the essence of this trend in her wallpapers of the 1970s and 80s, creating a nostalgia for times past. She brought a breath of the countryside to urban interiors with patterns of great simplicity and freshness, both in fabrics and in wallpapers, and developed a market world wide for a style which was seen as essentially English. It incorporated the most popular design reference of all – the flower.

This was part of a continuous tradition which had begun with the Tudor rose used as an outline motif in the very earliest of printed papers, and which reached its apogee in the plethora of flower patterns produced in the early nineteenth century. Even Morris and the Arts and Crafts Movement, who disliked the general run of wallpapers they saw about them, adopted the floral motif with enthusiasm.

Floral papers can create a soft and gentle atmosphere in a domestic setting, offering a relaxing and pretty contrast to the often bleak and minimal decoration of the workplace. Perhaps this is why, of all repeating patterns, those which take flowers as their inspiration go from strength to strength with every manufacturer producing large ranges of designs both traditional and modern.

DECORATING WITH PAPER

BORDERS, DADOS
& FRIEZES

The enormous range of wallpaper borders available today provides exciting opportunities for creating a different look – something far more individual in its impact than just plain walls or an uninterrupted expanse of wallpaper. Used in even the simplest, most restrained way, borders add an elegant and pleasing detail to an interior, as well as bringing a professional-looking finish. Used with imagination and panache, they have even greater potential for decorative innovation.

Borders have been used for almost as long as wallpapers themselves. Originally they were hung to conceal the tacks that held wallpapers in position, but by the late eighteenth century they had begun to assume real importance as a decorative feature in their own right. In addition to the many floral and decorative borders, which were very popular, a wide repertoire of architectural friezes and borders was produced. Many of these were printed to look like a cornice and hung at the junction of wall and ceiling to add importance and grandeur to a room.

By the beginning of the nineteenth century designs had become extremely elaborate and superb trompe l'oeil swags and festoons, also for use at cornice level, were supplied with a straight border that could be used for outlining doors, windows and walls. French manufacturers in particular produced very luxurious and opulent swagged designs – heavily fringed and tasselled velvets, festoons of silk caught in knots and adorned with flowers, foliage, ribbons and feathers (see opposite).

By the end of the nineteenth century, when it became fashionable to divide walls into three bold horizontal areas each with a different patterned paper, in the dado-filler-frieze formula (see page 80), borders were often used between them, providing the opportunity to introduce yet another pattern. This very intensely patterned decoration was gradually superseded by a simpler style in which the frieze became deeper and more dominant, often surmounting a discreet paper or just a tall wooden dado.

Twentieth-century revivals of interest have produced some imaginative approaches to borders, notably in the 1920s and 30s when an immense variety of styles and colours were both inexpensive and readily available. Borders with the edges cut to follow the intricacies of the design along one side were widely used. Motifs of fruit, flowers and foliage, often outlined in black, and vibrantly coloured, made a strong decorative impact and were much in demand for the enlivening effect they had on cheap and undistinguished papers.

Some of the most interesting borders available today are reprints of archive designs. Many are rich and theatrical in their effect and have

LEFT *Borders – whether plain or patterned, architectural, floral or swagged – bring style, emphasis and an impressive final flourish to a decoration. Use them to define space, suggest a period, highlight attractive architectural features, such as a pretty arch or chimney breast, or simply to pull the design scheme together. There is a huge range from which to choose, both traditional and modern.*

Some authentic period designs are also still available. The opulent blue festoon with grey roses, for example, is hand-printed from the original nineteenth-century woodblocks.

PREVIOUS PAGE *Indian chintzes have traditionally been fashionable in Europe and have inspired many wallpaper designs. This modern copy of an original paper at Temple Newsam near Leeds remains faithful to the original in colouring. Manufacturers today usually interpret archive designs in a variety of different colourways to suit a broader range of tastes.*

LEFT *A delicate hand-painted leaf and flower border is used lavishly to define each wall in this bedroom at Drottningholm, a restored eighteenth-century castle not far from Stockholm, Sweden.*

BELOW *A plain tobacco coloured border, cut from lengths of wallpaper, emphasizes and enhances the architectural features of this hallway. It follows the diagonal line of the staircase and curves around the arch at the end of the hall.*

great impact, but, if they are hand-printed, often from the original woodblocks, they carry a corresponding price tag. There are, however, plenty of inexpensive borders, many with coordinating wallpapers, with which to create interesting and attractive effects. Indeed this is an area of interior design where bold imaginative treatment can more than make up for a small budget. You can stick pieces up temporarily with Blu-tack or masking tape before making a final commitment but take care, when removing them, not to tear the paper.

DEFINING SPACE & ENHANCING PROPORTION

Borders are the simplest and most versatile means of defining space and uniting design elements and are most effective if they are planned as an integral part of the decorative scheme. The simple addition of a border around the top of a plain painted or papered wall can transform a room; not only does it give emphasis and character to the wall, it draws the eye

RIGHT *The hand-blocked wallpaper and matching borders were imported from France in the nineteenth century and hung in the Jumel Mansion in Harlem, New York.*

The border runs not only around the fireplace, along the dado and the top of the wall, but also frames the windows. This is a particularly attractive way of treating windows which are not curtained, turning them into a decorative feature in their own right.

BELOW *A bold neo-classical border provides an appropriately important finish to an unusually striking wallpaper.*

upwards, providing a balance with other elements – furniture, carpets, ornaments, and so on – which claim the attention at a lower level.

Borders are extremely useful for enhancing, or altering, the proportions of a room. A high ceiling can be lowered visually by the addition of a paper border at dado rail level. This also provides the opportunity of introducing a different patterned paper beneath, either for practical reasons – in which case it might be tougher, darker and more highly patterned than the paper above, in order not to show marks – or just for the visual pleasure of an agreeable combination of papers. Continuing the idea up the stairs in a hallway will add interest to an otherwise featureless expanse of wall.

A wide border or frieze pasted along the wall at picture rail level, will also reduce the apparent height of a room, particularly if the ceiling colour is continued down to the level of the border and a contrasting paper is hung beneath it. The same lowering effect is achieved by a wide border pasted next to the ceiling as a cornice. If it is not possible to find a wide border to match a scheme, a combination of two or three widths of the same border can look striking and original. Although in principle you should not be deterred from using a wide border simply because a room is small – hung imaginatively it could make an exciting decorative contribution – if the ceiling is very low, a wide border at the top of the wall would make it appear lower still.

Awkward or odd angles, a sloping attic ceiling, for example, can be turned to good advantage with borders outlining the angles to emphasize their quirky character. But beware of drawing attention to features that might be better underplayed, such as windows of different heights and sizes, an off-centre chimney breast, or an uneven ceiling in an old house. For problems such as these, rather than using borders, choose a form of decoration that will make them less noticeable: a busy floral pattern can cover a multitude of sins.

In rooms of elegant proportions one of the most pleasing treatments of all is to use the border like a picture frame, outlining the wall at its edges and drawing attention to the wall itself as a distinct unit that makes an attractive background against which to display furniture and pictures. A more flamboyant approach might take its cues from the past, using attractive borders to draw attention to the room's architectural detailing by outlining doors, windows, fireplace and even bookshelves.

As well as looking attractive, borders help to hide the tiny mistakes in paper cutting which often spoil the work of an inexperienced paperhanger and enable you to create a professional-looking finish. Practical instructions for hanging borders, dados and friezes are given on pages 176–179.

BELOW LEFT *The Gothic window dictates the position of these wide floral borders. They are taken around the wall from the window seat recess to form a slightly higher than usual dado, and a slightly lower than usual frieze. However, the strong horizontal division is offset by the striped wallpaper and by the picture which hangs very comfortably between the two bands.*

BELOW RIGHT *A coordinating border emphasizes the elegant proportions of this bathroom. It also breaks up a faux marble wallpaper, which might otherwise be overpowering, into attractively balanced areas. By taking the border along the top of the dado rail and into the curve of the arched window, the scheme is given a pleasing visual coherence.*

LEFT *The door frames in the Phelps-Hatheway House in Connecticut are constructed in a manner found frequently in late eighteenth-century houses. It was typical to take a border all round this frame, following the extended angles at the top, emphasizing the shape and giving more importance to the doorway. A paper border following the simpler lines of a modern door frame looks equally attractive.*

ABOVE *A border of pink and lilac coloured sweetpeas echoes the floral theme of the bedroom beyond and establishes a continuity which leads the eye comfortably from one room to the next.*

ABOVE RIGHT *The unusual branch detailing on this cast-iron fireplace (top) suggested an appropriately rustic leaf and twig border. It has been cut to give a naturally broken*

outline and carefully pasted to join around the corners, softening the otherwise hard edges of the fireplace.

A more formal version of the same idea is shown in a detail (below) from a fireplace in the Gardner-Pingree House in Salem, Massachusetts, built in 1804. The border design reflects the classical style of the fireplace and adds definition to the decoration of the room.

DESIGNING WITH BORDERS

The easiest way to choose borders and wallpapers which look good together is to consult the manufacturer's pattern books where coordinating borders are shown as variants on the design of the main wallpaper. The general intention is to take a single design idea and rework it in a variety of different ways. There are pretty florals to team with delicate sprigged papers, and richly ornamented patterns which develop the theme of the accompanying wallpapers. Plain or very discreetly patterned papers are presented with striking borders that give the paper more impact. Archive designs are reproduced in both their original versions and in modern colourways. These papers and borders are all carefully matched to work together, giving the chance to create visual variety and the confidence to know that whatever combinations you choose will look attractive.

When coordinating border designs are printed on the same background as the matching wallpaper, the join between the two is invisible once they are on the wall. Thus quite complicated design images may seem to flow freely around the top of the wall, just as if they were an integral part of the main wallpaper.

Coordinating borders and papers are easy to use, of course, but there is no need to follow the manufacturers' suggestions, and many original – and often far more interesting – combinations can be put together using borders from one source and papers from another.

To get an idea of the finished effect before embarking on a scheme, it may be helpful to take photographs and sketch in on them the various possibilities. This is particularly important if the room presents problems such as the oddly-shaped walls in this small bedroom in a converted barn.

Here it was finally decided to run the border like a frame around the walls. Behind the bed it outlines the wall area above the shelf. The border brings weight of colour and pattern to the edge of the wall, balancing the strong design of the coordinating bedcover and cushions.

ARCHITECTURAL BORDERS
Elements of classical design create convincing impressions of architectural mouldings. They range from simple beadings and carved rope effects to deep cornice friezes with richly modelled acanthus leaves.

The Greek key pattern (at the bottom of this page) provides a classic finish and is illustrated here in several different guises: it works effectively at ceiling, dado or skirting level.

The traditional egg and dart design (above the Greek key) is also shown in different interpretations. This

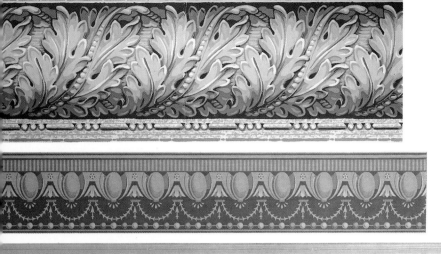

design is conventionally only hung at the top of the wall.

The cut-out pattern of interweaving circles (opposite page) contains floral motifs which recur in a more stylized form in the wider border below.

One of the most versatile for bordering, outlining and creating panels is the plain reed and crossed ribbon design.

Medieval Gothic architecture, with its familiar pointed arches and quatrefoils, is the inspiration for the final border below.

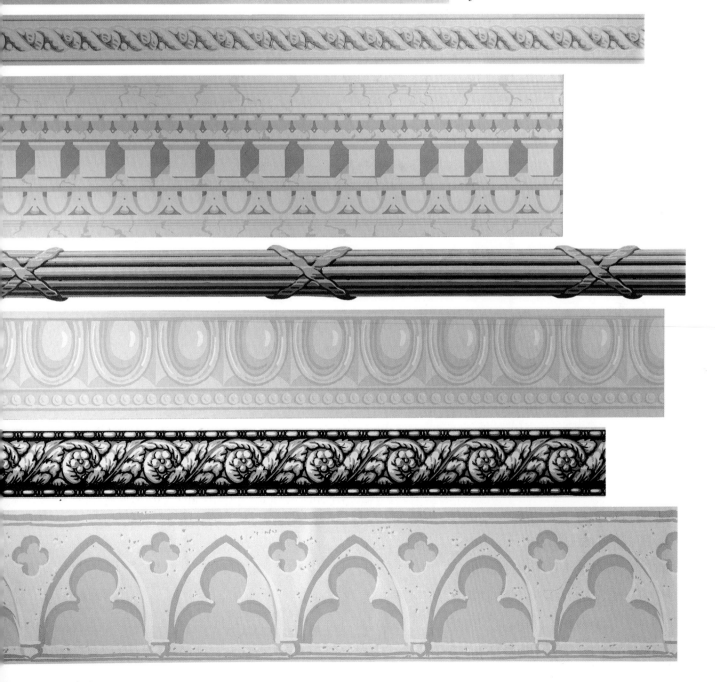

RIGHT *Two architectural paper borders are used in this Empire-style bedroom. The bold three-dimensional cornice is hung around the top of the wall, appearing to support the ceiling. The narrower border frames the scenic wallpaper like a picture. Depicting a scene from the myth of Cupid and Psyche, the panel was designed by Dufour in 1816 and subsequently reprinted by Zuber from the original woodblocks.*

BELOW *An architectural border printed in tones of grey to give a natural stone look defines this archway and the window beyond. Just above the skirting board the same border is used on a larger scale, bringing weight, balance and visual unity to the setting.*

ARCHITECTURAL BORDERS

Architectural borders are designed to look like the kind of moulded plaster decoration that was commonly used until the early years of this century to finish rooms in all but the most modest of dwellings.

Detailing of this kind is rarely found in modern houses and may often have been removed in older houses at a time when it was fashionable to take everything back to unadorned walls. It is possible, but very expensive, to replace plaster mouldings or to introduce them where none have existed. Fortunately, however, architectural borders are produced by many wallpaper manufacturers today, and they offer a much cheaper, but highly effective, substitute. They are usually based on the classical repertoire of design motifs, freely interpreted in different sizes from simple narrow beading to the wider egg and dart patterns and large scroll and acanthus leaf designs. They are often printed in convincing trompe l'oeil so that the paper gives the effect of standing proud from the wall. Additionally, there are borders of plain mouldings which can be used to create a dado rail or to outline doors and windows.

Architectural borders are most effective in natural colours: grisaille, cream, terracotta. If you wish to depart from the classical look and to create a richer-looking Victorian or Edwardian interior, more highly coloured designs are appropriate, especially the dark greens, rich crimsons and autumnal shades usually associated with those periods.

Where moulded decoration already exists on the ceiling, an architectural border can be positioned at the top of the wall to continue the theme. Because such borders represent a design detail which in certain settings would be taken for granted, they are visually unobtrusive while at the same time contributing significantly to the character of the room. A simple egg and dart motif in a small room looks appropriate. In a room with higher ceilings, you can be more adventurous, with a wider more flamboyant cornice design. While architectural borders are clearly not a suitable choice for rooms with wooden beams, or with very low ceilings, they can enhance the plain walls of modern houses, provided their scale is in harmony with the surroundings.

SWAGGED & FESTOONED BORDERS

Trompe l'oeil swagged and festooned designs, swathes of silk, flowers, laurel wreaths, tassels and cords offer exciting creative possibilities. In bold colours they can add a touch of drama; in quieter tones they add a softly defined delicacy.

Some opulent nineteenth-century borders, as well as some of the more delicate 1930s designs are still hand-printed in France, using the original hand-block technique which results in a thick, rich, slightly chalky colour. Many have been reinterpreted in colours that are more suited to modern tastes and, of course, it is possible, though costly, to commission such borders in colours to match a particular scheme.

These so-called 'document designs' are grand in their effect and need suitably high ceilings to accommodate them; but contemporary designers have adapted the theme in swagged borders that work well in the most up-to-date interiors. This type of elaborate border is intended

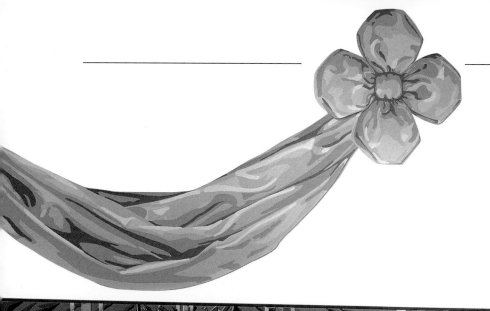

TROMPE L'OEIL SWAGGED BORDERS
These swags look even more opulent and dramatic on the wall, especially when accompanied by a simple paper. Most extravagant of all are the nineteenth-century French designs at the top and foot of the opposite page. Printed from the original blocks, they display the rich density of colour typical of hand-printing.

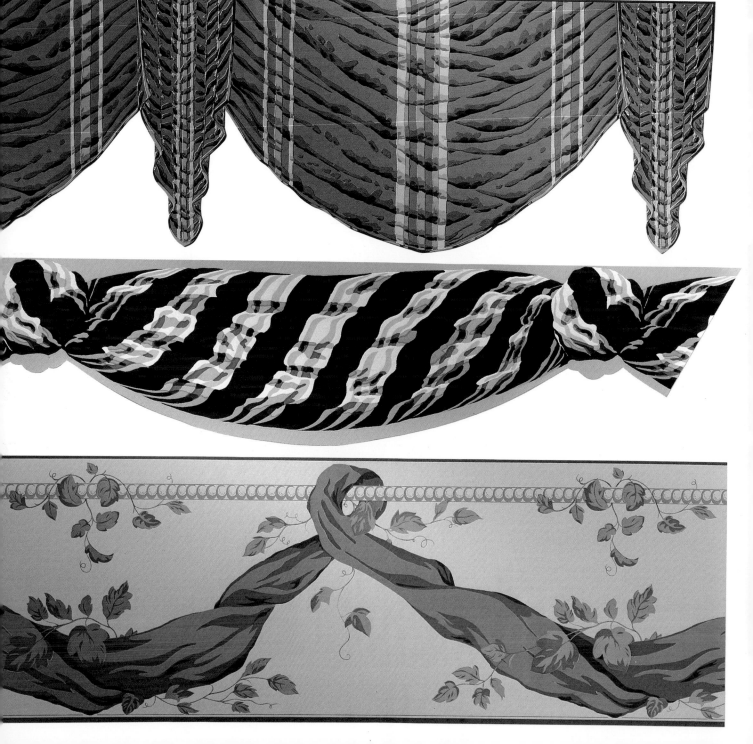

to make a strong design statement and in the past would have been used with a rich paper simulating draped fabric.

Some older designs are available with a complementary version in a narrower width printed beneath them on the roll. This is intended to be cut off and used either above the skirting board or at dado rail level, thus doubling the design impact of the border.

Most swagged borders should be cut out, and this is not difficult since the designs themselves are large. Problems may arise in hanging, for it is most unlikely that a swag will finish exactly in the corner. If this is the case, make sure that the most conspicuous corner is the one that is perfectly arranged by starting with that corner and working away from it. The problem does not arise with swagged and festooned borders which have been designed as individual pieces and are supplied already cut out. They are far easier to hang perfectly since they can be overlapped or arranged with gaps in between to fit precisely into the corners (see page 178). Gaps can be covered with rosettes or knots, and the effect is of a continuous trompe l'oeil border.

The simplest way of decorating with swagged borders is to use those that are printed on a plain background that matches the colour of the room's main wallpaper. The designs are often smaller than those that are intended to be cut out, but they can be pasted straight down: there is no need to cut them out. Borders like this look pretty in bedrooms where a softly draped feminine look may be required; in bolder colour combinations they look equally effective in living areas.

ROPE BORDERS

For sheer versatility, rope borders are hard to beat. They fit in anywhere, working as well in a modern town house as in a stately mansion or country cottage. While not necessarily imposing a style on the room – they bring a crisp, neat finish to the decorative scheme.

A wide range of different colours and designs is available, but it is not necessary to aim for a perfect colour match with the main wallpaper – a slight contrast is more interesting. Effects vary according to the colour combinations of the twisted rope, ranging from soft, muted tones to bold combinations of primary colours with a positively military air. The gentler colours look as good on a background of similarly restrained tones as they do on one that provides a stark contrast; the stronger shades look as effective on dark colours as they do on a lighter background.

Hand-printed rope borders are often supplied with two or more runs printed up together on one roll, rather than in one continuous length. If they are on a white background paper, they will look much better if, instead of cutting along the straight edge and leaving little triangles of white that spoil the effect, you cut away carefully around each 'scallop'. Of course this takes time, but the result, when seen on the wall, will repay the effort involved. Borders that are printed on a background colour that matches the main wallpaper do not need cutting and can be simply pasted up as a straight band. But easily the most striking three-dimensional effect is created by the trompe l'oeil borders which are supplied already cut out; when hung on the wall they give every appearance of thick twisted rope.

ABOVE *A deeply swagged border enriches the decoration in the long narrow hall of a London house. The same border, in a different colourway, is illustrated on page 71. Its intricate mix of ornamentation, with scooped pelmet, tassels and fringes, gives a clue to the mid-nineteenth-century origins of the design, which makes it an apt choice for a house of similar age.*

A simple rope border, in the same terracotta colour, is pasted beneath the dado rail and completes the decoration.

LEFT *When these borders are cut out to obtain a scalloped edge, they effectively imitate the rope trimming which was their original inspiration.*

FLOWER & RIBBON BORDERS

Flower designs have traditionally been such a popular source of inspiration that it is not surprising that there are masses of floral borders available. Teamed with a small sprigged patterned paper, they give a charming, rural feel; used with an almost plain paper printed in similar tones – a paint effect, for example – they give a more sophisticated look. While small floral designs in pastel colours are always popular and easy to find, contemporary designers are introducing a refreshingly new approach with motifs that are much freer, livelier, brighter and bolder. They work well with an equally strong wallpaper colour, and provide an exciting background for an adventurous concept of decoration that owes little to the gentle charm of the 'English country house style'.

Many floral borders are designed to complement particular wall-papers and, indeed, the design is often printed on the same background as the wallpaper it is intended to partner. The border leaves and flowers then give every appearance of having been cut out and hung on top of the paper. Bedrooms look especially pretty decorated in this way.

Colourful floral borders introduce the freshness of a country garden to the most urban interior, without the dominating effect of an overall floral wallpaper. Crisp designs in clear colours bring an attractive finish to a simple decorative scheme.

RIGHT *Original eighteenth-century borders outline an elegant fireplace. The narrower one is carefully and imaginatively cut to echo its intricate lines.*

BELOW *An unconventional use of borders introduces a note of sophistication in a country bedroom. Hung vertically, the French hand-blocked border of intertwined roses produces the effect of an ultra-wide stripe on the pale cerulean blue walls. Oval framed pictures visually interrupt what might otherwise have appeared too linear an arrangement.*

Hung in this way, the border takes on a major role in the decoration.

MAKING YOUR OWN BORDERS

With such a huge variety of borders available, it should be easy to find what you need, but you might like to try creating your own.

The simplest but quite often the smartest borders are plain bands that provide a contrast with the wallpaper. And while you can buy plain borders ready made, you may prefer to cut your own border strips from a roll of wallpaper.

The width of the strips need not be dictated by the size of the room, rather by the effect you wish to achieve. Wide, bold borders can make a dominant statement in a small room just as narrower borders can make a discreet statement in a large room.

One way of obtaining a really wide border is to use two contrasting plain borders, mounted one above the other. Use the one with the dominant tone on the outside, to define the edge. The easiest way to get a professional finish is to cut one wider than the other and paste the narrower one on top so that the wider one shows beneath.

Some border patterns can be given a new, much greater, impact by a little imaginative cutting. Geometric shapes and repeat patterns, for example, that are not particularly impressive in their original state, can be cut out following the line that draws attention to the strongest design element.

The most striking results may arise from the simplest, least expensive ideas. Striped wallpapers with a pattern or floral motif in between the stripes, have great potential for use as borders. If the pattern works

LEFT A clever compromise between wild extravagance and wily economy, this border illustrates Do It Yourself at its most imaginative. It is cut in long strips from a supremely luxurious French hand-blocked paper in which stripes alternate with rows of gilded and flocked motifs.

Individual strips define the walls and dado. At cornice level the improvised border is used in conjunction with the ornate border designed to accompany the original paper.

RIGHT One of the easiest and cheapest ways to create a border with striped paper is shown here. A narrow band is pasted around the top of the wall misaligning with the paper below by just one stripe.

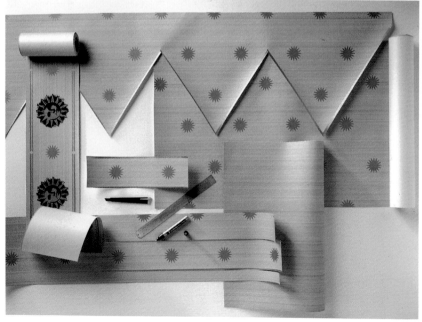

The imaginative use of simple papers transforms an ordinary hallway into an unforgettable one. A pale blue dragged paint effect paper covers the walls; another version of the same paper, printed with stars, is used on the ceiling. A coordinating border with gold and black suns completes the celestial theme.

Beneath it, another border, cut in bold triangles from the starry paper, hangs like pennants. The shape was first drawn lightly in pencil, then outlined in gold pen and finally cut out using a metal ruler and scalpel.

A simple border cut from strips of starry paper and edged thickly in gold adds a finishing touch to the corners of the wall.

horizontally as well as vertically, you can cut several widths from one roll of wallpaper.

A smart finish to a striped wall can be obtained very simply by cutting one complete strip from the side of a striped paper and hanging it horizontally between the top of the paper and the ceiling, just like a conventional border. Another strip pasted along the bottom will complete the effect. If you are using a paper with evenly spaced stripes, you can make a very different border by pasting a thin strip of the same paper at the top of the wall, just out of sequence, so that the pattern 'jumps' slightly. Again, this neat and interesting finish is very simply achieved.

Remember, too, that if you find a bold decorative motif that particularly appeals to you, perhaps in a design sourcebook, you can photocopy it. Enlarge it, if necessary, and copy it as many times as you need to make the required length. A black and white original copied on to a good quality coloured paper is striking. Suggestions for the most economical way of copying your source material, as well as instructions on hanging borders that you have produced in this way, are given on page 179.

ABOVE *An inexpensive way of obtaining large quantities of border is to cut up a roll of striped wallpaper into separate lengths. The pink and yellow rose design is printed three times across the width of the paper and can easily be cut into strips to give 30m/100ft of border from one roll. Even more lengths can be cut from a narrower stripe.*

LEFT *Photocopied motifs look particularly striking when printed on coloured background papers.*

DADOS & FRIEZES

A dado is a traditional method of dividing the wall space into separate areas and enhancing its proportions. Rising, usually, from the skirting board to about chair-back height, it divides the wall horizontally and serves both a decorative and functional purpose. As an architectural device for adding refinement to a blank wall it may be represented simply by a wooden or plaster rail marking the division or, more importantly, it can be an entire panelled section.

Wallpapers produced as dados were originally copies of panelling, designed to bring an inexpensive elegance to a room. Some were fairly plain, others might be filled with elaborate decorative rosettes and medallions. The dado papers designed to be used in conjunction with the splendid panoramic papers so popular at the beginning of the nineteenth century often represented suitably imposing balustrades that established the architectural boundary for the scene beyond. Some specialist companies today have original nineteenth-century dado designs that they will print to order.

Dados were often designed with matching 'friezes', most of which, until the late nineteenth century, were basically rather wide and elaborate borders: the majority were architectural in inspiration, though swags of flowers and draperies were also popular. Today a frieze usually implies a significantly wider border of the kind that assumed great importance in the final decade of the nineteenth century.

In the 1870s and 80s the Victorians, not noted for their restraint in matters of decoration, took every opportunity to indulge the fashionable taste for rich pattern. It was thought dull in the extreme to use one wallpaper only and preferable by far to introduce at least two other patterned papers – as dados and friezes – to sandwich a central expanse of filler paper. The proportions varied according to whim; dados, for example, were often taken considerably farther up than chair-back

Wallpapers inspired by original nineteenth-century designs are used in this restoration of a Victorian mansion in Melbourne, Australia.

The base of the decoration is the dado, a heavily patterned paper covering the lower part of the wall. A border divides it from the filler paper above – a simple design of repeating Greek palm-leaf pattern printed in gold on a pale celadon background. The theme is picked up on a larger scale in the wide frieze at the top of the wall.

*The dado-filler-frieze combination, so popular with the Victorians, is used here with pleasing restraint. In the past, however, as can be seen from the 1876 manufacturer's catalogue (*LEFT*), it presented opportunities for unbridled indulgence in a plethora of different patterns and colours.*

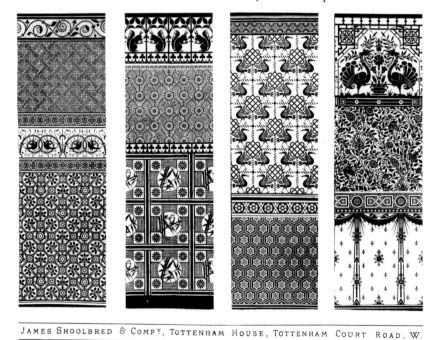

JAMES SHOOLBRED & COMPY, TOTTENHAM HOUSE, TOTTENHAM COURT ROAD, W.

As many as six or seven different patterns might be piled one on top of the other in the Victorian dado-filler-frieze combination. Though such mixtures of design and colour are unlikely to appeal today, a judicious selection of harmonizing papers makes for a lively and interesting decoration.

The hallway in this Edwardian house is decorated in authentic period style. A reproduction Lincrusta, heavily embossed with a characteristic stylized flower design, is painted the same green as the oakleaves on the wallpaper.

Lincrusta, which can be painted any colour you wish, is still a practical choice for the lower part of the wall, particularly in halls.

height, and friezes could be as deep as 1.2m/4ft, leaving a very narrow filler. Thus a great variety of decorative schemes was achieved, though such intense combinations of pattern on the wall tended to make rooms appear smaller and less formal. Sometimes the same papers, or even different ones, were repeated on the ceiling, creating a rich, dense, intricate effect which to modern tastes seems, to say the least, overpowering. Or is it simply that we lack the bravura of our Victorian forebears?

A more restrained version of the idea using different papers and borders can certainly look attractive today, but it is important to choose papers that complement each other in design and colour. A patterned dado, a plain paper above and two harmonizing borders, one at the top of the dado, one at the top of the wall, can produce an interesting combination, and some pattern books show wallpapers and borders already selected to work in this way. A plain dado with a pattern above is a more conventional combination, which can be enlivened with a striking border. Stripes, too, work well in this context, especially in halls and stairways when they are combined with a plain paper.

If you want to re-create an authentic nineteenth-century style dado there are many suitable designs to choose from. If the main purpose of the dado is practical – to withstand the wear and tear likely in a hallway, for example – then the sturdy Lincrusta, a linoleum-based material, or Anaglypta, a cotton paper, both very widely used in Victorian times, are still available. Both have a raised, patterned surface tough enough to stand up to most bumps and scratches.

ABOVE *Carved wooden dado rails still exist in the halls and landings of many nineteenth-century houses. Their pleasing upwards sweep provides visual interest in stairwells and they present the opportunity to break up a long expanse of wall by the introduction of contrasting papers.*

There are few specially designed dado papers available today but many wallpapers, particularly those with non-directional patterns, can easily be cut to fit this area. Instructions for hanging dados are given on pages 169 and 179.

The large repeating pattern of the full-blown roses on the dado wallpaper and matching curtains makes for an agreeable design unity in this hall. Easily the most eyecatching element of the decoration, it effectively contrasts with the restrained pink-striped wallpaper which has been hung above.

RIGHT *If there is no existing dado rail, a border can be used to divide the wall. In this skilful improvisation, a single border is used to create the panels, the dado 'rail' and the dado itself. The edging strip suggests the dado rail while separate lengths, butting neatly, are pasted side by side to make the dado.*

FAR LEFT *The translucent glow of the jewel-like colours in the 'Peacock Frieze', designed in 1900 for the Shand Kydd company, is more evocative of stained glass than of wallpaper.*

The 'Barclay Frieze' (BELOW), designed in about 1903 by William Shand Kydd, shows the influence of Art Nouveau.

LEFT *Wide landscape friezes hung at the top of the wall were popular in the early 1900s. This stencilled frieze was designed by Rex Silver.*

BELOW *A dramatic modern frieze, printed in one colour on a plain background, dominates this bedroom. It is designed to accompany the dado and border in the same colourway.*

By the last decade of the nineteenth century, the fashion for the multiple arrangement of the dado-filler-frieze started to wane. People began to prefer a simpler style of decoration in which the dado was virtually abandoned, while the frieze went from strength to strength. A discreetly patterned paper would be hung from floor to picture rail and above it was pasted a wide, boldly designed, brightly coloured frieze – the focal point of the decoration. As the fashion for friezes spread, many different, highly distinctive designs became available. Decorators could choose between the panoramic impact of a romantic landscape unfolding around the top of the room or a repeating pattern of flowers and foliage in the Art Nouveau manner perfected by the eminent wallpaper designer William Shand Kydd. While Shand Kydd's stencilled and hand-blocked designs represented the height of achievement in art wallpapers of the day, many other more prosaic frieze subjects were also available. Sporting motifs, nursery characters and storybook scenes were enormously popular, and there was scarcely a room in the house for which an appropriate frieze could not be found.

Such overwhelming popularity was bound, eventually, to produce counter reactions, particularly among those with pretensions to taste, which so often implies exclusivity. By the end of the first quarter of the twentieth century, moves away from the frieze were being encouraged by manufacturers who began to supply instead all the elements needed to make different arrangements on the walls: cut-out motifs, borders and cornerpieces that could be combined to create decorative panels.

Today only a few wallpaper companies supply beautiful wide friezes either as reprints of original designs or as fresh interpretations of the idea. However, if the type of frieze you want is not commercially available, it is always possible to improvise. One very simple way to get the effect of a strong decorative band at the top of the wall is to use the entire width of a suitable wallpaper, or to use a combination of several borders pasted one overlapping the other. Once again, the confidence to meet a challenge in an imaginative and unconventional way is likely to produce uniquely satisfying results.

PANELS

Paper panels made with borders and wallpapers add decorative distinction as well as formality and balance to a room. Simply by dividing the wall area into sections and outlining them with a paper border makes an interesting design statement that may need no further embellishment. But elegant panelling often seems to call for something inside it – and pictures, mirrors, plates, even light fittings may all be enhanced by being displayed in this way. In this case the border becomes a frame, like that of a picture, and it may equally well be used to surround an attractive wallpaper or a specially designed panel decoration.

DESIGNING WITH PANELS

Not only do panels add a new aesthetic dimension to a room, they can alter its apparent physical dimensions. As professional interior designers know well, dividing a wall up into different sections can minimize problems of height and proportion. A dado with horizontal panels, for example, will help lower a high ceiling just as a strong vertical panel arrangement breaks up a long expanse of wall.

Panels can be made in whatever dimensions are necessary to achieve an arrangement that is pleasing to the eye. They may be of identical width, but, to avoid a rigid uniformity reminiscent of a row of guardsmen, it is usually preferable to alternate wider panels with narrower ones. For a balanced look, make the space between and above them equal, even if the panels themselves are of different widths, but allow a slightly larger space between the bottom of the panel and the skirting board.

Panels impose certain constraints on any decorative scheme, simply because of the symmetry they introduce, bringing order to the walls and influencing the position of other decorative elements such as pictures and large pieces of furniture. But this should be regarded as a virtue rather than a problem because it helps reinforce the general feeling of balance which is one of the most attractive aspects of panel decoration.

In large, high-ceilinged rooms, usually found in older houses, panels fit easily and naturally: some such houses occasionally retain their original wood or plaster panelling, but if this architectural feature has been removed, architectural borders can be used to simulate moulded panels that help restore the room's former elegance. Plain or patterned borders would work equally well, though they would, of course, create quite a different effect. Smaller rooms with lower ceilings need carefully considered treatment, because panels might diminish their size. But there is no reason to be deterred, provided the decoration is kept simple and in proportion with the scale of the room.

Not only walls, but doors, screens and even ceilings can be effectively decorated with panels. Recessed panels in doors can be filled with an

Decorative paper panels may consist simply of an attractive border outline or they may be made to contain something – a picture or ornament, for instance, or a special wallpaper. Panels offer the opportunity to use small quantities of a very expensive wallpaper or to enjoy a design which might be overwhelming if it were used on all four walls.

attractive paper, or doors without any architectural detailing can be enhanced with paper panels that may match the paper used on the walls. This can be particularly important in a bedroom where a blank wall of fitted cupboards can break up the decorative theme. A paper door panel can be neatly finished with a narrow border either in a complementary colour or in a matching design. Alternatively, a thin architectural border that looks like beading or moulding can be used to complete the panel effect.

The decoration of the ceiling is often neglected in contemporary fashion. In the past ceilings received just as much attention as walls – often even surpassing them in the extravagance of their embellishment. Today, however, most people simply paint them white, or off white, and leave it at that. But they provide an ideal opportunity for more adventurous treatment, especially with panels and borders. By outlining the edge of the ceiling you can introduce some colour to an otherwise plain expanse of white, or, if the ceilings are reasonably high, they can be decorated with panels of patterned paper, perhaps continuing or developing further the theme of the walls.

BORDER PANELS

The simplest panels are basically an extension of the border concept. If you paste a border all round the perimeter of a wall some distance from the edge, you create, in effect, one large panel. By outlining further subdivisions of the wall, you can create a number of smaller panels, both vertical and horizontal. A discreet border simply defining a panel shape on a subtly patterned or textured paper would contribute the same kind of understated elegance as would either traditional wooden panelling or plasterwork.

Variations on this theme can be tried with papers of slightly different colours or tones within and outside the panels. If the same colour is used, a different finish inside the panel would also work well: a fabric effect paper, such as a damask or a moiré, or one with an interesting paint effect, would add a new dimension and depth. These approaches, however, are rather restrained, creating a quiet and undemanding background. By contrast, papers and borders chosen for the richness of their pattern can be a great visual stimulus, inspiring the rest of the room decoration and creating a unique, personal style.

RIGHT These elegant border panels are made from a simple narrow strip trimmed from the edge of a wider, patterned border paper.

When planning an arrangement like this, which depends so much for its success on balance and symmetry, the placing of all elements has to be considered from the outset. Careful thought has gone into the positioning of lights, wall-hung plates and furniture.

The restrained panel design and the softly muted colours, of traditional Scandinavian inspiration, combine to produce an atmosphere of uncluttered calm.

BELOW A variety of solutions to the perennial problem of how to cope with a long, narrow, featureless hallway are illustrated in The Book of the Home *published in England in 1925. As well as the introduction of pattern in the dado, panels are suggested as an effective and interesting means of breaking up the wall surface. Modern versions of these ideas, using up-to-date wallpapers, present far more exciting ways of hanging wallpaper than the conventional wall-to-wall, floor-to-ceiling approach.*

1. Chinese Decoration   2. Patterned Dado and Border with plain filling   3. Panelling effects by patterned borders on plain papers

CORNERPIECES

Some of the prettiest panels are made by using borders with matching cornerpieces, which add a delightful finishing touch to the arrangement. Many of those available today take their inspiration from historic designs, interpreting the theme of the accompanying border; others are new designs using the same elements in simpler ways.

As with so many attractive ideas in wallpaper decoration, few manufacturers have exploited the virtue of cornerpieces and you may find them difficult to track down. It is quite easy, though, to make your own. All those on the right were cut from wallpapers or borders with suitable motifs.

LEFT An antique border with a strong green and coral design creates distinctive panels which 'frame' the family portraits. This is a bold treatment in a small room, but an imaginative one that brings an ordered symmetry and decorative focus to the walls.

BELOW LEFT A wide geometric border panel provides further definition for the picture.

BELOW RIGHT Classical-style panels give a dull flat door a new look. The Roman head and the urn were enlarged from smaller motifs and photocopied on brown paper to achieve an antique finish.

PANELS AS FRAMES

If border panels are to contain pictures it is obviously important that the pictures are enhanced by the arrangement. There should be enough space around each picture for it to look balanced. If the picture frame overlaps the panel side it will look awkward, so the size of the panels should be decided by the width of the pictures.

Pictures often have much greater impact displayed in groups rather than being dispersed individually around the room. One panel containing perhaps two or three pictures, flanked by two empty panels, may look more effective than three panels with a single picture. Grouping pictures in panels offers an ideal opportunity to develop a specific visual theme. If you decide to do this you can tap a variety of sources: a collection of inexpensive prints, from a book or an old calendar, for example, might form a suitable basis. They can be pasted directly to the wall in the manner of a print room (see pages 122–141): the prints in the Pompeian hall shown on pages 96–97 were trimmed, so the white surround would not spoil the effect of the decoration.

Panels outlined with borders can equally well be used, of course, to display other decorative wall-hung objects. But choose the borders carefully: if they are too eyecatching they will detract from the impact of the central display.

A POMPEIAN HALLWAY

Strong design images of ancient Pompeii are combined with colours that evoke the warmth of southern Italy. The decoration looks rich and rare, but it is not difficult to achieve.

Two brushed paint effect wallpapers in slightly different but harmonizing earth colours are used: the pinker toned paper covers the walls, and the coral colour is used for the panels. The central panel is made from the full width of the paper, slightly narrower widths are used for the side panels.

The wide hand-printed border that frames the panels has a strong classical motif in black; this is balanced at the top of the wall and along the skirting by the bold interpretation of the Greek key pattern.

A collection of classical prints is pasted directly to the wall. The designs are adapted from decorated vases found at Pompeii when it was first excavated in the eighteenth century and the overall effect is reminiscent of Pompeian wall paintings.

Chairs with painted backs depicting similar motifs continue the classical theme. The table, however, is very much of the present and illustrates how well antique and contemporary styles can blend.

PANELS WITH DECORATIVE PAPERS

As well as creating the illusion of a panel by defining a space with a border, panels can be made specifically to contain and outline a particular wallpaper. There is an interesting historical precedent for this approach: in the eighteenth century wallpaper manufacturers such as Réveillon produced designs that were distinctive enough to be displayed in this way, as well as papers that were specifically intended to be hung as panels.

Certain wallpapers lend themselves beautifully to the panel treatment and they can be used to transform or enliven a plain or simply patterned background. Papers of contrasting colours, patterns and textures, papers that are simply too exotic, too rare or too expensive to be used in great

ABOVE *With his supremely refined decorative innovations of great technical virtuosity, Jean-Baptiste Réveillon revolutionized eighteenth-century wallpapers. This panel is typical of his finest work.*

RIGHT *The exotic style of the Ottoman Empire is captured in a rich and intricate panel using different but complementary papers and borders. The designs are based on sixteenth-century Turkish tiles.*

Similar effects could be achieved using paisley borders and wallpapers, combining different designs to emphasize the eastern influence in their complex patterns.

quantities – all can look superb. By displaying a paper in a panel you draw attention to its special qualities. The intrinsic beauty of a hand-blocked design, for example, can be enhanced by hanging it in a panel where its impact is not diluted by over-repetition of the design motif.

If you choose an intensely patterned floral design, a small-scale repeat or a larger pattern that is complete over the width of one roll, the width of the panel will probably correspond with the width of the paper. In other papers, a major part of the design may fall on the edge of a roll, to be continued in the next drop. In this case a join can be made in the panel and the outside edges trimmed to the required width. A variety in panel width is not only more interesting, it allows you to select different parts of certain designs to make up the panels.

Choosing from a coordinated range put together by the manufacturer will ensure that borders and papers team successfully. But you may wish to be more enterprising and mix papers and borders from different sources. In the absence of pattern, papers can be cut to virtually any shape you wish, enabling you to move beyond rectangular or square panels and to introduce diamonds, triangles, circles, ovals and curves. The impact of the panel relies on the colour of the paper and the shapes created, and marble or paint effect papers are ideal for this kind of design treatment (see pages 102–103).

The character and texture of the furnishing fabric and curtains are reflected in wall panels filled with a blue-grey damask paper. As a quiet contrast, the remaining wall area is painted a soft yellow.

The success of this traditional treatment arises from the sensitive use of subtle, closely toned colours which provide a pleasing background for the ornate gilding and the antique mahogany furniture.

A CLASSICAL REVIVAL

Reproduction Réveillon wallpapers, with characteristic arabesques, urns and festoons, produce an elegantly feminine effect in this bedroom. Jean-Baptiste Réveillon was an eighteenth-century wallpaper manufacturer whose superb hand-blocked designs found great favour both in his native France and in North America.

Many of his papers were specifically intended to be hung in panels, not relying on overlapping patterns to create their decorative effect. Narrow panels with simple designs were printed to hang together with larger, more complex panels, the space between being filled with plain paper.

In this bedroom two distinct but complementary designs form panels of different widths. The larger panels are made up of a width and a half of the first paper, the smaller panels from half a width of the second, as shown below. They are surrounded by a contrasting border of formal geometric pattern, which is also a reproduction of an original Réveillon motif.

The background paper is a subtle moiré (see also page 16).

RESTATING THE PAST

Some of the most exciting design ideas take their inspiration from the past, and the imitation marble panels in the eighteenth-century music room at Segerhof in Switzerland (right) provided the stimulus for this strikingly modern decoration.

Marble panelling has a long pedigree – it was an important feature of classical interiors – and its beauty resides in the colours of the stone as well as in the shapes in which it is cut. The classical model has been reinterpreted at Segerhof: marble wallpaper, printed in England, forms elegant panels, complete with decorative medallions.

Natural stone finishes are popular today, and there are many *faux* marble papers available. Several different types – from extravagant hand-printed papers to inexpensive machine-made versions – are used in the panels on the left.

It is sensible to begin working out a design like this on a small scale, cutting up pieces of paper to make a miniature version of the panel before committing yourself on a large scale. Experiment with their size and position on squared paper, then pencil an appropriately enlarged grid onto the back of the marble wallpaper to cut, for example, the diamond shapes. The circle can be drawn to whatever diameter you wish by fixing a piece of string the length of the radius to a drawing pin at one end and a pencil at the other. The circle is used as a template for the semi-circular panel edges. This design is quite complex, but much simpler schemes can look equally effective.

LEFT *Eighteenth-century Chinese papers, with characteristic hand-painted flowering branches, birds and foliage, grace this drawing room at Svindersvik in Sweden. Originally intended to run continuously as a panorama around the room, they have been hung here in separate panels with ornate gilt mirrors and windows in between.*

BELOW *Chinese craftsmen still practise traditional painting skills and these four interlinking drops from a modern paper incorporate the most popular elements of antique designs. They can be hung together in a continuous panorama or split to form panels.*

PICTORIAL PANELS

Beautiful hand-painted Chinese papers have traditionally been displayed in panels as well as in continuous panoramic decorations around the room, and in many historic houses it is still possible to see them hung in this way.

If the idea of a Chinese scenic paper appeals to you, and yet the thought of decorating an entire room seems overwhelming, panels provide the perfect solution. Importers of hand-printed Chinese designs, at the luxury end of the market, are usually prepared to sell just one set, of four to six panels, which can be hung together, split into smaller groups or hung individually around the room. If you anticipate moving house and taking these special panels with you, have them professionally mounted on light wooden battens that can be removed from the wall.

While modern European and American wallpaper versions of Chinese designs are roller printed, and thus have repeating patterns, they can be treated in the same way, creating a pretty effect of *Chinoiserie* quite inexpensively. Arranged in twos or threes on a plain background, they introduce a delightful Oriental atmosphere. They may be hung like pictures or pasted to the wall and surrounded with paper borders; bamboo border designs would be a particularly apt choice.

Wonderful scenic panels, which exploited the exuberantly illusionistic techniques in which they excelled, were produced by French manufacturers at the beginning of the nineteenth century. Called *décors*, these were less ambitious than panoramas, which filled the entire room, but were nonetheless far larger than any picture you would expect to find in a domestic setting. Hundreds of rich and vibrant colours were used in their production so that, even on close inspection, it is difficult to believe that they are not painted by hand. They depict scenes of lush vegetation and gardens full of flowers, or sometimes romantic landscapes or scenes from classical mythology. The viewer is transported into a world of illusion where a trompe l'oeil vista opens out from the room. Paper columns, pilasters, cornices, balusters, dados and friezes were used to frame the panels and suggested the edge of the room, while the landscape on the panel stretched out into the distance beyond. But eventually these architectural features assumed greater importance and became so decorative that the subject they framed could be left out altogether and panels were created using just the pillars, dados and friezes.

Scenic panel decoration became popular again between the First and Second World Wars, when the subjects, usually landscapes, were printed in far fewer colours. This made them considerably less expensive and therefore more widely available than their predecessors.

Many people today like the concept of scenic trompe l'oeil, but it is not always easy to track down. If you wish to pursue the idea you may be able to obtain the elements you need from a specialist company; some produce modern versions of the garden scenes so popular in the past, while others produce trompe l'oeil columns and colonnades (see page 117). As is so often the case, a daring and imaginative approach is likely to produce exciting results. You may find some interesting ideas in the chapter on Wall Decorations (pages 108–121) that you can use as a springboard for your own design.

'Armida's Garden', one of the most celebrated of the extravagant French décor panels, was awarded a medal at the 1855 Paris Exhibition. This large panel – a colourful and voluptuous expression of unruly horticultural delight – is the central part of a design incorporating smaller side panels. It measures 3.89 × 3.37m/12¾ × 11ft.

A modern trompe l'oeil garden panel transports the viewer past elegant topiary to an idyllic view of distant lakes and mountains.

WALL
DECORATIONS

When walking round the older parts of any large city your attention is likely to be focused on the many distractions at street level – shop fronts, people, traffic. Yet a glance upwards may be richly rewarded, for it is likely to reveal, on buildings more than fifty years old, an astonishing wealth of decorative architectural detail. Buildings without such embellishment are a relatively recent phenomenon and many of them are now widely disliked, not only for their size and their uncompromising profiles, but because they present such a plain face to the world. There is no relief, nothing to entertain the eye.

Highly ornamented façades were once commonplace in both public and domestic architecture, and were by no means confined to grand buildings. By the end of the nineteenth century decorative devices in stone or plaster were being mass produced and builders could order the elements they wanted from catalogues crammed with a vast range of ready-made architectural ornament. Thus the doors and windows of even quite modest houses came to be flanked by classical pillars and topped by a fine cornice or triangular pediment, while additional embellishment might be introduced by stylized flower garlands, wreaths, flowing ribbons and bows. This was a continuation of a tradition that favoured an elegant finish as a way of bringing character and style to a building.

Such ornamentation was, of course, as important a feature of interiors as it was of exteriors. At its simplest, decorative plasterwork was used to describe the structure of the room, in the form of moulded borders or friezes. In grander houses, however, it was used to decorate the wall surface with large and elaborate motifs often taken from classical sources. In eighteenth-century England this sort of decoration ranged from the formalized panels, trophies and friezes in the style of Robert Adam to the exuberant swirls and asymmetry of the Rococo, with its strong Chinese influence. Even more opulent decoration can still be seen in stately homes and palaces whose walls and ceilings are decorated with complex and lavish scenes incorporating three-dimensional figures and often feature little *putti* disporting themselves against a background of puffy white clouds. The motifs were not always classical, however, and the Victorians also turned to medieval styles for decorative inspiration: Gothic ornament is characteristic of the second half of the nineteenth century in both interior and exterior decoration.

In houses that were not graced with three-dimensional decoration, similar effects could be achieved with paper ornaments printed as highly convincing trompe l'oeil pastiches of moulded plasterwork and carved

Trompe l'oeil wall decorations can be used to create magical illusions. Most of these paper ornaments are presented already cut out, so they can be combined in many different ways. They may be used to create a focal point, perhaps over a fireplace or, more adventurously, to create a style for a whole room.

wood. They, too, were available in a wide variety of designs and decorators could create their own arrangements from collections of motifs which were supplied in sheet form ready to be cut out and pasted to walls and ceilings.

Later different styles of paper ornament evolved. Cornerpieces for panels, little pictorial vignettes, oval medallions in decorative cartouches and geometric shapes were produced to add interest to otherwise plain walls. Elaborate borders with an intricate cut-out bottom edge were combined with these elements. They were fun to use and brought a pleasurable degree of individuality to the decoration. By comparison the approach to decorating walls with paper in the post-war years seems singularly dull and unadventurous. But fashion is dictated to some degree by availability, and, until recently, the necessary elements for this kind of decoration simply have not been available.

Now some specialist companies are reproducing archive designs and others are introducing fresh interpretations of traditional ideas. Among the latter are the trompe l'oeil decorations illustrated here and on pages 112–115, which take their inspiration from architectural themes and

ABOVE *The ceiling of a tiny square bathroom is enlivened by trompe l'oeil cut-out decorations. Flying cherubs, linked with garlands and bows and pasted against a blue-grey paper, appear to cavort about the sky.*

*The same trompe l'oeil elements are used in a very different way on the screen (*RIGHT*) which creates a charming decorative focus in this dressing room. The cherubs could also be used with bows and garlands to make an effective arrangement over a door or an archway – both areas with decorative potential that is rarely exploited nowadays.*

from the kind of decorative motifs that in the past were rendered in stone, stucco, plaster or wood.

USING PAPER ORNAMENTS

Paper ornaments are supplied already cut out and are intended to be used in a variety of ways. You can either set the theme for a room, using a range of elements to achieve the effect, as has been done in the Gothick room illustrated on page 26, or you can use a few pieces to decorate chimney breasts, alcoves and recesses, or, indeed, any area which you want to make a focal point. If you begin working with paper cut-out decorations on a small scale and are pleased with the result, this may give you the confidence to attempt a more ambitious room setting later.

Garlands of fruit and flowers linked with rosettes form a swagged border beneath the cornice in this drawing room. The arrangement over the fireplace finishes with two drops in a similar style, creating a focal point on the chimney breast. The area is further embellished with bows and ribbons from which the small oval portraits appear to be suspended.

A CLASSICAL ROOM

Trompe l'oeil trophies representing Art and Music set the theme for an elegantly classical room in the eighteenth-century manner. Pasted to a plain wallpaper background, these cut-out elements stand out clearly, just as white-painted plaster relief decoration contrasts with a coloured wall. They look equally effective against a wallpaper with a simple brushed, dragged or sponged finish.

Trophies carved in stone grace the façades of numerous classically inspired buildings. Many incorporate military symbols, reflecting their origins in Ancient Rome when soldiers hung their breastplates and helmets on their spears in an arrangement intended to represent victory and military might. When trophies, rendered in plaster, began to be widely used in interior decoration, other themes were depicted as well. They represented more peaceful pursuits, such as Art, Love, Music, Poetry and similar diversions of the Enlightened mind.

Art would be symbolized by a painter's palette, rolls of paper and paintbrushes; Love by a pair of doves surrounded by flowers; Music might incorporate an arrangement of instruments and sheet music.

The idea has been adapted in the trophies shown here, which, once seen hanging on the wall, look extraordinarily like the plasterwork which inspired them. Several could be hung to create a dramatic theme for an entire room or, alternatively, just one could be used to introduce an element of visual surprise in a hallway or at the end of a corridor.

The panel outline is first marked lightly on the wall in pencil, and then the pieces are hung temporarily in place with Blu-tack, to check that the arrangement is satisfactory. Individual motifs can be trimmed or overlapped as necessary to fit the panel size. In the case of the lower panels they are cut slightly smaller to give the required depth; an alternative would be to overlap them and cover the joins with rosettes. The central motif consists of three pieces — the bow, the ribbon drop and the trophy.

A MODERN TENT ROOM

The success of this tent room results from the effective combination of striped wallpaper, carefully mitred on the ceiling, and the convincing trompe l'oeil paper ropes. The pale blue stripes evoke the awnings of marquees erected for summer festivities, and bring a light-hearted sunny feeling to the room. A combination of white stripes with any pale colour would have a similar effect, while deeper, richer combinations of reds, greens or greys would create a far more formal, military style.

Whether the final result resembles more a marquee, a campaign tent or even a tent in a bedouin encampment, clearly depends on the colours chosen. But the paper alone is not enough – the rope border is an essential element in achieving a convincing 'tent'. Straight rope borders are used to emphasize the joins on the walls and ceiling, but what brings such panache to this room is the swagged rope border hung to look like a pelmet.

The trompe l'oeil swags and knots are all separate elements, put together here to make a border, but with the potential for a variety of other uses. Straight pieces are combined with rosettes and tassels and arranged to look as if they are supporting the plates and pictures.

There is much amusement and satisfaction to be had from designing the arrangement that works best in your room. Perhaps the more formal pelmet border illustrated above, with 'U' shapes rather than swags, would be appropriate. These pieces work in the same way as the rope swags, overlapping to fit the length of the wall exactly, but create a more structured look suitable for the more serious environment of, say, a study.

In kitchens, where much of the wall space tends to be occupied by shelves and cupboards, the tent-room effect gives an opportunity to introduce an interesting decoration at ceiling level. Even small rooms, such as bathrooms and cloakrooms, can look very effective decorated in this way. And the tent-room treatment can turn a hallway, which might otherwise appear rather dull and featureless, into an area of character and interest.

Cut-out trompe l'oeil swags, such as those used in the tent room, opposite, can be used in any arrangement you like.

The pillars, swagged cornice and striking classical dado are printed on separate sheets, ready to be cut out and tailored to individual settings – much as they would have been in the nineteenth century. The columns are printed on a background and can be used as panels or cut out and adjusted to fit the height of the room. Their spacing is dictated by the divisions in the dado beneath.

These elements provide a wonderful opportunity for creating a formalized panel decoration embellished in the traditional manner.

COLUMNS & COLONNADES

As well as trompe l'oeil architectural details simulating moulded plaster or carved wood, other more elaborate architectural elements were produced in paper in the nineteenth century. Columns and colonnades were used with great imagination and daring, and were an essential framing element for trompe l'oeil scenic panels.

Similar large-scale architectural elements can be obtained today and demand considerable assurance and boldness of vision if they are to be used successfully. Some columns are available already cut out with a choice of orders to finish the top; you may opt for the formality of the Ionic capital or the relative exuberance of the Corinthian, with its stylized acanthus leaves. Whichever you choose, the effect will be dramatic. Columns are also available printed in combination with architraves and borders which together can be used to make panels.

Decorating the walls of a kitchen with a trompe l'oeil stone balustrade or the walls of a study with columns capped with authentic classical orders may seem like the ultimate *folie de grandeur* and inappropriate in a conventional house. But trompe l'oeil can make light work of formality and create a dramatic decoration without grandiose overtones.

A three-dimensional balustrade, which appears to support the breakfast bar, and pictures hung with cut-out ribbons and chains transform a kitchen-dining area into a stylish and original room. Running along the top of the wall, a bold architectural border gives cohesion to the scheme.

Balustrades around the lower part of the room make an interesting variation on the dado theme. The background to this reproduction, hand-printed nineteenth-century dado paper has been partly cut away so that the paler wall colour shows through the spaces, creating a convincing impression of a free-standing balustrade.

A GRAND ILLUSION

The wit of trompe l'oeil turns a bachelor's study of quite modest proportions into a classical 'folly'. This slightly 'tongue in cheek' treatment illustrates how effectively trompe l'oeil decorations can create an illusion that is entirely removed from everyday reality.

Columns of positively Athenian splendour appear to support the ceiling, while the grey-blue wallpaper sprinkled with puffy clouds draws the eye beyond them, suggesting a feeling of lofty spaciousness. A balustrade gives balance to the design and provides a reassuring boundary to the room.

These are wallpaper ornaments on a large scale and need a very positive approach to maximize their design potential. You can go the whole way and create a room around them or just use a couple to frame a doorway.

The column shaft can be shortened, if necessary, to fit between skirting board and ceiling. This room already has a plaster cornice, but you can easily improvise with one of the architectural borders shown on pages 66–67.

Columns are available in different sizes; the terracotta one on the right would fit well in rooms of moderate height, but the stone coloured column is on a much grander scale. Wider, and with a weightier base and capital, it looks effective with a ceiling height of 3m/9ft or more.

The climbing ivy adds a romantic touch at the same time as softening the stark vertical fluting. It was cut from a roll of wallpaper that features trails of ivy along its length.

Making your own wall decorations is easy once you develop an eye for the kind of papers that can be cut up to provide the necessary elements.

Several different papers are used in this design: one roll of trellis wallpaper, one roll of trailing ivy, several rose-patterned borders and a blue ribbon cut from a roll of paper (a length cut from a flower and ribbon border would have done equally well). Each of the flowers in the central arrangement has been cut and pasted on individually.

MAKING YOUR OWN WALL DECORATIONS

If you are working on a small scale, you can either use specially designed wallpaper decorations or you can cut your own motifs from rolls of wallpaper. Bring your imagination into play when leafing through the pattern books; some exciting possibilities may occur to you. But be selective and only choose motifs that are well designed and printed. Good designs in strong colours that already have an effective three-dimensional appearance are more likely to be found in expensive papers or borders, but as you will only need small quantities there is no need to feel inhibited about cutting them up.

ABOVE *An impressive arrangement of full-blown roses and symbols of Love is designed to hang as an overdoor decoration. Carefully cut away from the background on which it was supplied, it has great visual impact. The gold border beneath follows the frame of the door.*

The area over the door, usually ignored in modern interiors, presents the opportunity for developing a variety of decorative ideas. An adaptation of the floral motif illustrated on the opposite page, for example, using flowers cut from wallpapers and borders, would make an original design.

RIGHT *This pretty little orange tree, complete with Versailles tub, is printed in France to an old design. It is supplied with an accompanying trellis border and panel background, so that several panels can be linked, if wished. The original background has been cut away to make this attractive focal point, which creates the feeling of a conservatory. It would be an amusing and decorative addition to a real conservatory or sun room.*

PRINT ROOMS

An original, highly individual way of decorating walls that is currently enjoying a revival of interest is to cover them with prints in the manner of a print room – one of the more whimsical decorative inventions of the eighteenth century. Formal reception rooms were covered from dado to cornice with a collection of prints, not conventionally framed and hung but cut out in a variety of shapes – circles, octagons, ovals, rectangles – and then pasted directly onto the wall. Against a light background wall colour, usually buff, straw, or shades of white, they were arranged in carefully balanced groups. Printed cut-out paper borders pasted round individual prints gave the illusion of frames. The overall effect was of a crowded but elegant picture gallery, with the formality enlivened by the addition of cut-out paper swags, garlands of flowers, printed ribbons and classical ornaments pasted around the prints to link groups and create a decoratively pleasing composition.

Making a print room is an enjoyable way of creating a very personal decoration, and this, no doubt, is one of the reasons why the fashion was originally adopted with such enthusiasm. Nor is it difficult to do, whether you choose to decorate in authentic eighteenth-century style or decide on a more up-to-date interpretation of the idea.

While early print rooms would have been hung with black and white engravings or mezzotints, an authentic look can be achieved today with reproductions, though it is still possible to come across inexpensive original prints. But do not be afraid to cheat a little if you wish: good photocopies can be given the patina of age by the use of cold tea, and will look quite convincing once in place. The choice of subject matter is virtually limitless. Apart from the traditional Old Master subjects, landscapes and architectural vistas, there are portraits of the famous and infamous, kings and courtiers, actors and musicians, and prints depicting every possible subject from ballooning to botany, from marine life to fashion.

A single subject or theme can provide the inspiration for an entire room. Alternatively a disparate collection of prints will bring variety and interest. Obvious places in which to search are shops specializing in the sale of old prints, but antique shops and stalls are also a good source. An entire collection of similar prints could be taken from an existing book. Though you might be reluctant to break up an old book for this purpose, many old prints will, in fact, have been derived from this source. The most unlikely place may yield an exciting discovery and a few more prints to add to a growing collection.

In the eighteenth century, black and white engravings were cheap and plentiful, and if colour was required it was often painted in by hand. Many of the antique engravings found today have been coloured in this way only recently and to the purist eye are spoilt. But if you are not

In the prettiest print rooms an imaginative mixture of prints is framed and linked by paper borders and other decorative elements – large and small, simple and ornate. These can be cut from specially produced sheets incorporating large numbers of borders and other motifs. Cutting out, arranging and rearranging them until you achieve the perfect combination is an engrossing and pleasurable pursuit.

attempting historical authenticity it is effective to adapt the idea to a more modern idiom and use contemporary coloured prints.

Today colour printing is inexpensive so it is simplicity itself to make a collection of pictures, posters, or prints in full colour to create a modern interpretation of the print room. It is important, however, to choose prints which harmonize in both colour and style. A selection of botanical prints taken from a calendar, for example, can provide the basis of a delightful decoration. Prints such as these may often be enhanced by a variety of different coloured cut-out borders chosen to complement the scheme of the room. You can make even simpler borders by mounting the prints on coloured paper and then hanging them with bows and ribbons cut from a roll of wallpaper.

Large prints can be framed effectively using conventional wallpaper borders but the borders should be cut to finer widths, if necessary, so as not to overwhelm smaller ones. Cutting modern prints in a variety of interesting shapes, in the traditional manner, will help create a lively composition. Those that have a white background can easily be cut into circles, octagons or diamonds without spoiling or encroaching on the subject matter. Experimenting like this can be great fun, and you will

ABOVE *Even bathrooms can be given the print room treatment. The size and subject matter of these large prints – photocopies of Piranesi engravings – call for wide, bold frames and cornerpieces. Their impressive formality is agreeably counterbalanced by walls painted a sunny dandelion yellow.*

RIGHT *A print room decoration on an unusually strong background colour transforms this hall into a bright and welcoming space. The archway, its most arresting feature, is enhanced by the linked circular prints hung to echo its shape. They are crowned by a group of garlands and bows, a motif which is repeated over the groups of prints on the other walls.*

FAR RIGHT *Botanical prints form the basis of this collection. They have been skilfully hung as a uniform group along the top with a balanced arrangement of different shapes and sizes beneath. A narrow print border edges the walls and emphasizes the pretty arched window frame.*

ABOVE *A variation on the eighteenth-century print room theme was created in the library of Leixlip Castle in Ireland in 1976. The visual impact of the prints comes from their unusual shapes and the subtle balance of their arrangement.*

LEFT *Making a print screen allows you to experiment with ideas on a smaller scale. In this handsome example, a rich velvety red makes a vibrant background to an imposing group of prints. Screens can serve a practical purpose in keeping out draughts or hiding things you do not wish to see, as well as being decorative.*

achieve an unusual form of decoration and a very personal interpretation of the print room concept.

As in the past, the idea can be exploited virtually anywhere in the house, though it is particularly effective in small rooms. It is also an attractive way of decorating a hall or staircase where pictures often look awkward, hanging at different levels going up the stairs. Use cut-out paper decorations to link the prints in pairs or groups to create a more unified impression. This is also an idea worth adopting for a child's nursery or playroom. Postcards, prints, calendars, birthday cards and favourite reproductions of children's book illustrations can all provide material that is pleasing to arrange, and a source of delight for children.

EIGHTEENTH-CENTURY PRINT ROOMS

Collecting prints is – and was – part of the pleasure. In the eighteenth century many were acquired on the Grand Tour, a cultural tour of the major cities of Europe, particularly those of Italy, undertaken by young gentlemen, and others of independent means, who wished to extend their classical education. Just as the modern tourist returns with postcards and colour prints as reminders of paintings seen, say, in the

Prado in Madrid, or the Louvre in Paris, so no visit to Florence or Rome was thought complete without the purchase of several prints of classical ruins or of Renaissance works of art.

At the same time printmakers in London and Dublin were reproducing many different kinds of paintings in print form, so there was considerable choice without venturing overseas. These black and white engravings covered an immensely varied range of subjects. As well as reproductions of Old Masters, classical and mythological scenes and architectural views, there were all manner of statues, busts and urns, readily available and inexpensive enough to be cut up and pasted permanently to the wall. Responding to demand, the same printers also produced specially designed sheets of borders and decorative devices which were used to embellish the prints.

The inspiration for the print room is thought to have come from Italy, where scholars and noblemen would sometimes have the tops of a wall decorated with a frieze of black and white etchings, interspersed with small bronze statues. It was Lord Cardigan who was credited with introducing the idea to England. From his collection of fine prints he selected enough to cover the walls of a small room and framed them with specially printed borders. This was the room that inspired Horace Walpole, an eighteenth-century writer and connoisseur with a passion for decorative innovation, to create a print room at his home at Strawberry Hill outside London. He described it in a letter to a friend as 'a bedchamber, hung with yellow paper and prints, framed in a new manner invented by Lord Cardigan, that is, with black and white borders printed'.

Lord Cardigan started a vogue for creating print rooms which was to last for more than seventy years, but which seems to have been principally confined to England and Ireland. That the fashion may have crossed the Atlantic to New England is suggested by an advertisement, dated 1784, proclaiming that one Joseph Dickinson of Philadelphia was available to 'superintend or to do the business of hanging rooms, colouring ditto plain or with any device of prints, pictures or ornaments, to suit the taste of his employers'. But no print rooms survive in North America.

Some print rooms were created by professionals, others were made by the house owners themselves and can still be seen in their original setting. One of the oldest surviving rooms is at Castletown, a large classical house in Ireland. It is thought to be the work of Lady Louisa Connolly who arrived there as a young bride at the age of fifteen. She clearly found great pleasure and occupation in the decoration of the house and – since it was usual for aristocratic ladies of the time to become accomplished in the decorative arts – it was natural that she should have undertaken the print room project herself. Lady Louisa was obviously not very interested in architectural ruins and almost all the prints are figure compositions reproduced from Old Master paintings. Several of the portrait subjects are surrounded by pretty oval and circular frames and the prints are arranged in groups linked with garlands of flowers and printed ribbons. Interspersed among the prints are intricate trophies of dead game, a reference, perhaps, to the sporting pursuits of the family.

LEFT Lady Louisa Connolly created one of the prettiest eighteenth-century print rooms at Castletown in Ireland. She cut the prints in a variety of shapes – octagons, ovals, circles, squares – and arranged them in distinct groups, using printed paper embellishments to create a highly decorative arrangement. Garlands and bows crown the larger groups while swags and ribbons link the pictures below. Within the groups there is a great degree of symmetry with pairs of smaller prints balancing larger ones.

Grouping prints – rather than pasting them in a more random fashion over the entire wall area – is an approach that can be successfully adopted today.

BELOW Collecting prints is a particularly pleasurable aspect of creating a print room. In the eighteenth century, engravings depicting the ruins of Ancient Rome were particularly popular subjects, and were often acquired in the course of the Grand Tour. Here the same subjects are used to evoke the spirit of an eighteenth-century print room in a modern setting.

Though the painted wall on which the prints are mounted has now aged to a rather dull cream, it retains a freshness which enhances the prints and ornaments.

Thomas Chippendale, far more widely known for his cabinet-making than his association with paper hanging, is thought to have created more than one print room. An itemized bill for work carried out in 1762 at The Hatch, a country home in Ashford, Kent, certainly shows his involvement in this kind of decoration. As well as charging for materials, inter alia, '180 ft of Papie Mashie Border Painted Blue and White, 506 Printed Borders, 103 festoons, 74 Knots, 28 baskets and 8 Sheets of Chains' Chippendale charged for labour. By far the largest part of the bill, as may be imagined, was for 'Cutting out the Prints, Borders and Ornaments and Hanging them in the room complete'.

Though prints were traditionally pasted on a neutral coloured background, it was decided to paint the walls blue in the restoration of the print room at Ston Easton Park near Bath in Somerset. Like many other print rooms originally created in the eighteenth century this one had suffered over the years from the effects of damp. Fortunately, old photographs were available showing the room in better times, and these were used as a guide when the room was restored in the 1960s. Ston Easton is a perfect example of the delicacy of early print rooms.

An unauthentic but pretty blue was used in this restoration of the print room at Ston Easton Park in Somerset. The combination of large prints at the top of the wall with several tiny linked medallion prints below is also unusual, though faithful to the original. The effect is to draw the eye upwards, creating an impression of height and space in what is quite a small room.

While a highly ornamented, decorative look characterized the early print rooms, by the beginning of the nineteenth century the general impression was far more restrained and austere.

The Duke of Wellington, on his return to England in 1815 fresh from his victory over Napoleon at Waterloo, was presented by the British government with a large sum of money to purchase a country estate. He chose Stratfield Saye in Hampshire, previously owned by Lord Rivers, who had created a magnificent print room in the gallery, using Shakespearian characters as his subjects. The room inspired the Iron Duke to make several print rooms of his own in the bedrooms and in a small sitting room. It is not surprising that the latter has a military theme: uniformed soldiers, battle scenes, the Duke himself and even a print of his old foe Napoleon fill the walls. There are no delicate chains, garlands or ornamental devices to add lightness to the design: the scheme is rigidly symmetrical, a very different, though none the less interesting interpretation of the print room concept.

MODERN REVIVALS

Gradually the enthusiasm for print rooms began to wane, and it was no longer fashionable to decorate an entire room in this way. Few original print rooms have withstood the passage of time, and there are only about fifteen still in existence. However, over the last thirty years there has been a growing interest in their restoration. When the National Trust decided to re-create the flood-damaged print room at Blickling Hall in Norfolk, they made careful copies of all the original bows and

LEFT *Lord Rivers' print room in the gallery at Stratfield Saye. Interspersed among the scenes from Shakespeare are portraits, both contemporary and classical. Some are cut out in outline, others in ovals and octagons, bringing an interesting visual mix·to the composition.*

RIGHT *A circular print of the Wellington shield is the focal point in a print room at Stratfield Saye made by the Duke of Wellington himself. It introduces variety to an otherwise strictly ordered and formal arrangement.*

borders as they were removed from the walls. This had a happy consequence for would-be creators of print rooms as the copies became available from the National Trust, printed in black on cream sheets, ready to cut out and paste.

Similar sheets, reproduced from the Castletown print room, have been produced by the Irish Georgian Society. These were not available when the print room was created in the library at Leixlip Castle, County Kildare, in 1976. Yet so successful is this particular room, so harmonious and light in its arrangement, that it inspired many others and rekindled interest in print rooms in general (see page 127).

CREATING A PRINT ROOM

Several small companies and designers today will make print rooms to commission in the eighteenth-century manner. The prints may come from the client's existing collection or they are found specially for the project. It is not necessary to provide a 'period' setting: many new print rooms have been created in contemporary settings, where their style contrasts quite happily with more modern furnishing. While an experienced professional can produce excellent results, it is, without doubt, more satisfying to follow the example of Lady Louisa Connolly and enjoy creating one's own print room.

A well-developed sense of balance is required to create a unified composition on four walls, even in the smallest room. For this reason it may be sensible to restrict your first attempt to one wall only. After you have done this you will be in a better position to judge what is required when decorating an entire room in this way.

To start with, you need to have a fairly clear idea of your final design

LEFT *A circular frame can be made by photocopying, cutting and pasting curved borders from a print room sheet. The coat-of-arms was photocopied and cut to shape.*

BELOW LEFT *Bows, cornerpieces and border strips are used to frame and support this eighteenth-century print. It was picked up inexpensively in a rather battered condition from a mixed collection and shows Burlington House in Piccadilly, now the home of the Royal Academy of Art. When pasted, the folds disappear and the frame conceals the tattered edges. If the print were precious, it would be a simple matter to photocopy it and preserve the original.*

BELOW *A modern interpretation of the technique uses a reproduction print and a wallpaper border. The bolder effect is enhanced by the trompe l'oeil bow and ribbon.*

so you can obtain enough prints to fill the space. It need not be expensive to put together a collection, and the important thing is to be generous in the number of prints chosen. Nothing looks more mean or sparse than too few prints spaced about a wall supported by a meagre number of bows and drops, and it would certainly be more effective to cover just one wall than to spread available material too thinly over four. Choose a variety of shapes and sizes so the prints can be grouped in different ways.

Cutting out all the borders is quite time-consuming and sharp scissors and a good cutting knife are essential. A hard surface, such as glass, marble or metal is useful as a cutting board, and a metal ruler is invaluable for cutting straight lines. You will need a spirit level and tape measure in order to position the prints accurately.

The walls of the print room may be painted, or covered with wallpaper, so long as it has a fairly plain finish. Choose a wallpaper with an untextured surface otherwise the prints will not adhere to the wall.

A TRADITIONAL APPROACH

If your prints are new and you want to make them look older, simply make some tea in the usual way and when it has cooled submerge the print in it very briefly or wipe the surface of the print gently, being careful not to get too much liquid on it at any one time.

Once you have collected the prints, you will need a large selection of borders for framing them. As mentioned earlier, several companies produce printed sheets of borders and decorative motifs, or there are design sourcebooks which include all the bits and pieces that you will need. They can be photocopied and enlarged from the book, and repeated as often as necessary to produce the required quantity. Some

wallpaper manufacturers print classical borders suitable for cutting up into frames. These are usually too wide for any but the largest prints, but the design elements can often be cut into narrower strips so one roll of border can provide many metres of frame. Experiment with the most suitable borders to fit the size of your prints.

DESIGNING WITH MODERN PRINTS

A print room using modern prints in colour can be designed in much the same way as the traditional room, but you may prefer to use simpler borders than those made available on published print room sheets. Wallpaper borders are often suitable, and can be chosen to complement the colours of the prints. It is best to select fairly simple designs. Some borders showing architectural mouldings work well, but they may need to be cut down so as not to overpower the prints. You can create variations by using Italian marbled paper, cut into strips, to make borders. Some subjects look best with a plain border, rather like a mount, and this is very easy to hang. Cut a plain piece of coloured paper slightly larger than the print, and paste the print on top of the paper, allowing an equal border all round. Then print and border are pasted together on the wall.

With coloured prints it is better to use coloured bows and ribbons to provide the additional decoration. Some manufacturers produce wallpaper patterns or borders from which suitable bows can be cut, or you can use wall decorations which are already cut out.

HANGING THE PRINTS

There are several different ways to go about pasting and hanging and as you proceed you will probably develop your own method. But as a starting point the following is effective. Start by cutting out all the prints and borders. However much border is cut, you are almost certain to need more; it is difficult to judge the amount until you are arranging it and then you will be surprised by how quickly it gets used up.

ABOVE *The patina of age can easily be faked. Here decorative elements are photocopied from a print room sheet, dipped in cold tea for a few seconds then left to dry. The paper becomes slightly crinkly, but smooths out once pasted.*

RIGHT *A print with a beautifully hand-marbled mount, instead of a border, is pasted directly to the wall. Decorated with cut-out cherubs and garlands, the effect is original — classical, yet modern.*

FAR RIGHT *Favourite nursery prints or posters combined with simple borders make a unique decoration in a child's room. The pictures can be hung from specially designed bows or from ribbons cut from suitable wallpapers and borders.*

CREATING A MODERN PRINT ROOM

In this print room, reproduction botanical prints taken from a variety of sources, including old calendars and magazines, are framed with different wallpaper borders, shown below. Some are used in their entirety, others are cut out or trimmed.

The hand-painted Gothic design, for example, is trimmed to make a pretty border for the two largest prints. The hand-painted ribbon and bow border, cut out in long strips, frames the walls and provides bows and ribbons for hanging the prints.

Cut the borders with mitred corners: this can be done quite simply by folding the border over at an angle of 45 degrees and cutting along the fold, but to be certain of a good finish only mitre one side. Leave the other side straight and paste the mitred corner over it. How to mitre borders is explained in more detail on page 175.

Start by placing the biggest prints on the wall. Begin with the most important position, which will usually be over the fireplace, or on the wall opposite the window. At this stage attach the prints to the wall with Blu-tack so you can alter the placing easily. Achieving an attractive result is usually a question of trial and error, of arranging and rearranging the prints until they are successfully grouped. Think in groups of pictures, and try to avoid equal spacing between groups as this creates a less pleasing effect. Balance, however, is vital. The easiest way to achieve a balanced design is to use pairs of prints, starting with one large central picture flanked by smaller ones above and below, or side by side. Add the borders next, making sure that the frames do not overpower the pictures. Finally add the decorative details – for example, ribbons and chains to link the prints, bows to hang them, and a selection of trophies and ornaments to embellish the whole group. Again, time spent creating the composition is the most vital aspect of making a harmonious design, so continue to experiment until you are completely satisfied; then leave the arrangement for a day or two to be sure it works. Make tiny dots on the wall to mark placements when you remove the prints for the final pasting.

First dampen the prints with a wet sponge on the wrong side and then apply ready-mixed wallpaper paste or a starch paste. If the paste seems too thick and lumpy, add a little water. Make sure the paste covers the piece completely, especially the edges of intricate designs. Let the print absorb the paste briefly and then remove any excess with a soft cloth. Place the print on the wall, smoothing out any air bubbles with a soft cloth or paperhanging brush. Then hang the borders around the prints and finally paste up the bows, chains, ribbons and swags. Do this before the paste has dried on the borders so the chains and ribbons can be tucked underneath the edges. If you have covered a wall in a busy area such as a hall or stairway, you can protect them by varnishing the entire wall when the prints have dried. Use an acrylic varnish, as oil will discolour the paper.

USING FRAMED PICTURES

When a collection of prints is too precious to be pasted directly to the wall, or you wish to make a decoration which you can take with you when you move house, you can still create a print room effect with mounted and framed prints, hanging them in groups and decorating with swags and bows. A specialist framing company will make frames in a variety of shapes, so you can design the arrangements using square pictures, octagons, ovals and rectangles. The grouping of the pictures is important, but they will obviously be too heavy to experiment with Blu-tack on the wall. A practical solution is to plan the arrangement of both pictures and decorative paper elements on the floor. Measure the distances between the pictures. Hang the most important picture and

RIGHT *A collection of classical figure prints arranged in formal harmony on a warm ragrolled background lends a theatrical touch to this bathroom. A coat of varnish protects the prints from steam.*

BELOW *A group of French prints is beautifully framed and hung in the print room manner. The frames make for a much more substantial and weighty effect, which is complemented by the convincing three-dimensional appearance of the bows, swags and ribbons.*

then arrange the others around it according to the measurements you have taken. Once you are sure that the picture hooks are in the correct place, you can temporarily remove the pictures while you paste the paper decorations on the wall.

THE PRINT ROOM EFFECT

If, ultimately, you consider cutting and pasting, arranging and decorating too time-consuming there are quicker alternatives. In the eighteenth century, wallpapers were printed to look like a print room and similar papers are produced today. All the prints, garlands, bows, chains, borders and other decorative elements are already printed on a coloured background. Wallpaper printing techniques cannot possibly achieve the finesse of copperplate engraving, and, clearly, the opportunity for self-expression is removed – but it is an easy shortcut to the print room look.

Perhaps the most unusual interpretation of the print room concept today is a series of wallpaper panels with a textured surface that resembles a stucco wall, overprinted with a loose design of empty frames. These are linked with a free interpretation of ropes and bows, while along the base of the design there runs a series of rectangles which form a dado. The panels can be put together in different combinations and, if necessary, spaced out between doors and windows. Hung unembellished it is an amusing and lighthearted decoration, but it takes on a new life when prints are chosen to fill the frames. You could create an interesting and unusual gallery full of modern prints in this highly stylized setting.

ABOVE *An eighteenth-century block-printed print room wallpaper, found at Doddington Hall in Lincolnshire.*

OPPOSITE LEFT *Two modern reproductions of eighteenth-century print room papers. The one at the top was originally hung in the Lady Pepperell House in Maine.*

OPPOSITE RIGHT *A modern print room wallpaper that retains the spirit of the idea in the texture of the finely engraved lines. Beneath it is a luxurious hand-printed wallpaper designed in 1990. The separate elements could be cut out to suit your decoration.*

RIGHT *'Décor: Print Room' a Zuber wallpaper printed with empty frames gives a new twist to the print room concept.*

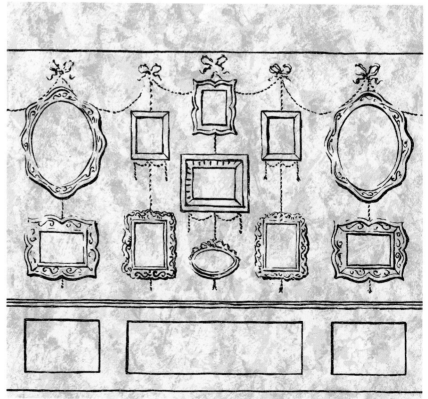

FINISHING
TOUCHES

DECORATIVE
ACCESSORIES

Many ideas for decorating walls can be adapted to add pleasing finishing touches to a wide variety of objects, including furniture. Attractive papers can also be used to line drawers and cupboards and to cover small items, from storage boxes to *cache pots*. Not only wallpapers and borders but wrapping papers, with their rich bright colours and infinite variety of designs, can be used when working on a small scale.

COVERING BOXES

Everyone has bits and pieces that need to be tidied away out of sight and boxes often make the most convenient containers. If they are to be visible, perhaps on a desk or shelf, there is no reason why, as well as providing a solution to an untidy clutter, they should not be made into decorative objects in their own right. Although finding pretty little boxes for trinkets, paper clips, and so on, is not difficult, larger boxes that are pleasing enough to be on display are less easy to come by. But many purchases come packaged in boxes which make excellent containers.

LEFT *Practical and pretty, these hat boxes can be displayed as attractive accessories. Each is covered with a different wallpaper and some are finished round the lid with a decorative border.*

PREVIOUS PAGE *Papers such as this beautiful Italian hand-marbled paper can be used for covering a wide variety of decorative objects.*

RIGHT *Bandboxes, originally used in the eighteenth century to contain the linen or lace neckbands worn by gentlemen, had much wider uses in the nineteenth century. Packed with small articles of clothing, ribbons, lace and bonnets, they were regularly used by travellers as alternatives to large trunks.*

They were highly decorative. Many were covered with scraps of colourful wallpapers while others — like two of the American boxes shown here — were embellished with specially produced scenic papers. Often bandboxes were used by manufacturers to advertise their wares, just as stores give away carrier bags emblazoned with their names today. The patriotic eagle on the top box holds a ribbon in its beak broadcasting just such a message.

LEFT *Many everyday objects lend themselves beautifully to covering with paper. Hand-marbled papers, an extraordinarily convincing malachite wrapping paper and a tapestry-design wrapping paper cover these obelisks and boxes.*

ABOVE *A group of desk accessories covered in marbled paper makes an elegant contribution to this bedroom with its superb panoramic wallpaper.*

RIGHT *The same kind of scenic paper used for bandboxes embellishes this nineteenth-century American spice chest.*

Shoe boxes, which are easy to obtain, are a good choice. Old file or document boxes which are capacious and strong can also be given a new lease of life with an attractive paper covering. More difficult to find, but perhaps the most desirable, are hat boxes.

The classic hat box is round, covered with vertical stripes, finished with a band round the edge, and lavishly ribboned – there may even be a hat inside it, for there is no better way of keeping one in perfect shape and dust free. But hat boxes themselves are so pretty that you may wish to use them as work boxes, perhaps to store tapestry, sewing or knitting. Covered in an appropriate paper, one or two will lend a charmingly extravagant air to any bedroom. Covering them is not difficult and offers the opportunity to experiment on a small scale with ideas that might be too complicated to contemplate on the walls of a room. You could use a lavish paper, since you will not need very much of it, or add an opulent finishing touch to a cheaper paper with small quantities of the kind of expensive border that is bought by the metre rather than the roll. Instructions for covering boxes are given on page 182.

Not only boxes but all sorts of other objects, such as wastepaper baskets, lamp bases, picture frames and desk sets are suitable for covering. In Italy there is a long and flourishing tradition for using paper in this way and the hand-marbled papers still produced by craftsmen in Venice and Florence are used to cover a huge variety of decorative objects. While these lustrous sheets of marbled paper can be purchased, it is also possible to make your own, from specially produced kits. The basic technique relies on the fact that oil and water will not mix. Tiny blobs of oil paint pigments are floated on a shallow bath of water, the surface is gently agitated with a feather which, as it passes from top to bottom and side to side, creates the characteristic wavy line effect. The paper is then floated on top and absorbs the pattern.

If you can cover a small box, there is no reason why you should not cover a much larger one, and a new paper finish might make a refreshing change on an old painted trunk or stripped pine chest. In the past blanket chests were often covered with patterned papers and can sometimes still be found in antique shops, looking rather tatty and just waiting to be covered. Those with domed lids make an especially pretty base. Deal with each side as a distinct entity and cover it with wallpaper using borders to outline the edges like a picture frame. Depending on the paper chosen, you can create anything from a Renaissance chest to an exotic Oriental box or just a boldly decorated container to hide toys away. If it is to stand up to a lot of wear and tear rather than to be merely decorative, then it needs to be finished with two or three coats of matt varnish to protect the surface and prevent the edges peeling.

PAPER LININGS

Having decorated the outside of a box, why not carry the idea through to the inside? A pretty lining paper makes it a surprising pleasure to open a box, the delight being in the discovery that someone has devoted thought to finishing parts of an object that are not normally on display. A chest of drawers or a cupboard could equally well benefit from the same final flourish.

LEFT *Portfolios covered in an Italian paper and a collection of boxes, transformed by various wallpapers and borders, reflect the musical and classical interests of the owner. The pleasure in covering boxes as a present for someone else lies in selecting a subject of special appeal to the recipient and creating a design around it.*

BELOW *Small shelves covered in marble paper create a fittingly opulent setting for a display of precious objects. Decorative squares at the joining point of the shelves give the effect of marble inlay.*

An old pine chest is lined with a modern copy of a seventeenth-century, block-printed paper. The coloured areas would originally have been hand-stencilled.

Papers such as this and the other reproduction seventeenth-century papers shown below, were frequently used to line trunks and Bible boxes as well as to cover walls and ceilings. Some, such as the two in the centre, took their inspiration from blackwork, an early form of English embroidery in which black silk was used to embroider linen.

One of the earliest recorded uses of decorative printed paper, in the sixteenth century, was to line trunks and Bible boxes. From fragments that remain it is clear that, since paper was then such a scarce commodity, a sheet that had originally carried a printed text might subsequently be reprinted with a design on the back. Designs usually featured small repeated patterns incorporating heraldic devices, Tudor roses, stylized flowers and leaves. They were printed on small sheets in black outline, showing the influence of blackwork, a popular form of embroidery at the time.

Today, when deciding on suitable patterns for lining papers, these early versions may provide inspiration. A small-scale motif is preferable to a large-scale pattern when it is used in small quantities and seen from a variety of angles. If you have a passion for authenticity, and wish to reline an old chest or trunk or create an antique character in a new one, choose a modern reproduction of one of these old lining papers.

The same small-scale designs would be equally attractive for lining the inside of cupboards but a larger pattern could also be used to take advantage of the extra space. As a contrast, try a paper with a bolder or more colourful design than that used on the walls, especially if the cupboard has glass doors through which it will be glimpsed.

Lining boxes, shelves and cupboards may be a more intricate procedure than hanging wallpaper but, as the pieces of paper are smaller, they are easier to handle. It is certainly worth taking time not only over your choice of paper but also over its application if the results are to be an enduring pleasure. Instructions for lining are given on page 183.

DECOUPAGE

The French word *découpage*, meaning cutting out or cutting up, gives its name to the art of decorating objects with cut-out paper motifs. These are arranged carefully, glued to the surface and then covered with many layers of varnish, making the edges of the paper invisible. The result resembles an exquisite hand-painted decoration.

Découpage was first employed in the seventeenth century by Venetian cabinet-makers who used coloured prints as a cheaper and quicker alternative to skilled hand-painting to decorate their work. In England the technique was known as 'japanning', for it produced a convincing imitation of Oriental lacquerware at a time when every-thing from the East was in vogue and demand far outstripped supply.

Among the gentry and nobility of eighteenth-century Europe découpage was enthusiastically adopted as a pleasant and rewarding pastime. It appealed particularly to ladies who enjoyed gentle pursuits which focused on the embellishment of their homes. By the nineteenth century, however, a more robust manifestation of the idea had developed. Gone was the finesse of finely cut-out intricate designs of flowers, fruit and foliage; découpage was replaced by scraps, a particularly Victorian passion.

Traditional eighteenth-century découpage continues to flourish, particularly in the United States, where its popularity is well established. Professional craftsmen produce beautiful and highly sought-after decorative furniture in the extravagant Rococo and *Chinoiserie* styles, and enthusiasts have developed novel approaches to the art.

Découpage can be used to good effect on many different objects: trays, screens, lamp bases and shades, *cache pots*, desk accessories, picture and mirror frames, even small pieces of furniture. While items decorated in this way look as if they are the work of a talented artist, in fact the skill involved is quite easy for anyone with patience to acquire.

Once you have decided what to work on, you have the pleasure of creating the decoration. As well as specially produced sourcebooks which reproduce original découpage archive material, greetings cards, gift wrapping papers, postcards and coloured prints will provide suitable motifs. It is best not to use photographs or prints with glossy surfaces, and pictures taken from magazines are also unsuitable because the print on the back of the picture will eventually show through and spoil the effect. If you are colouring in a black and white image, seal it before cutting it out in order to strengthen the paper and prevent the colours from running.

Patience is needed to cut out intricate subjects, but, with a good pair of scissors and a scalpel, it is not difficult. Choosing the best pieces and making a successful arrangement is obviously the most important part of découpage, but the design will evolve from the shape of the particular object and the decoration you wish to create. A tray, for example, can be treated almost like a picture, with a central motif surrounded by a cut-out frame. If the object to be decorated is a piece of furniture, a chair back, for example, or a small table, the technique is the same but the choice of design will relate to its position on the object. On a chair back a central arrangement might extend outwards on either side; on a circular

This modern bedhead is decorated with traditional Victorian-style découpage.

The decorative art of découpage can be applied to a wide range of objects. The technique is simple – cut-out paper motifs are arranged in an attractive composition, pasted to a surface and given between twelve and twenty coats of varnish. Each coat is allowed to dry then sanded down before the next is applied. The rich, lustrous surface that results is reminiscent of Oriental lacquerwork.

A large wooden box is decorated with an imaginative découpage of works by the eighteenth-century French artist François Boucher. It illustrates perfectly the wisdom of sticking to a single theme for a harmonious result.

table a continuous arrangement round the edge would leave scope in the middle for a bold motif.

Once the pieces have been glued in place the varnishing can begin. Between twelve and twenty coats are normally applied, each coat being rubbed down lightly when dry with glasspaper, so this is definitely not a pastime for people in a hurry. More detailed instructions on making découpage are given on page 183.

DECORATIVE SCRAPS

Making scrap screens, many of them intended for the nursery, was a popular Victorian pastime, and those that have survived provide fascinating insights into popular interests and amusements of the day. The scraps, usually highly coloured embossed motifs, could be purchased quite cheaply in sheet form, some already cut out. They were widely collected from about 1830 onwards and were used not only on screens but also to cover trunks and boxes and, most popular of all, to stick in albums specially produced for the purpose.

Unlike découpage motifs, scraps made no pretence at being anything other than themselves – and this less intricate, less time-consuming use of paper cut-outs was particularly appealing when decorating larger surfaces such as folding screens or cupboard doors.

Today the scraps can be cut out from posters, glossy magazines, postcards, inexpensive prints, calendars, or even wallpaper, and then pasted down in an orderly confusion of colour and subject matter. The arrangement works best if the scraps overlap at the edges and some of the pieces are cut out to outline the design, rather than cutting them all out in perfect rectangles. Give the piece a protective coat of varnish if it is likely to have to withstand being moved frequently.

A scrap screen made today will be fascinating to a future generation; it might even become a family heirloom. In the meantime it can serve a functional purpose as well as being highly decorative. It may act as a room divider or be used to conceal the untidy heaps that tend to accumulate in children's rooms.

LEFT A collection of beautiful découpage boxes, some of which clearly owe their inspiration to the print room. They were first lined in hand-marbled paper, finished at the edge with a border and then covered with a collection of prints.

ABOVE This modern scrap screen took shape over the course of several years as appealing pictures were discovered to add to the collection. Some are pasted on in their entirety, others have been cut out to give visual variety.

An arrangement could equally well have been planned around a single favourite subject – as was done on the Victorian nursery screen (LEFT). The scraps were bought as sheets, with the subjects already cut out.

SILHOUETTES

These are named after Etienne de Silhouette (1709–69), one of Louis XV's ministers, whose hobby was cutting portraits at lightning speed from pieces of paper. He started a fashion which quickly gained in popularity. Enterprising itinerant portraitists soon picked up the skill and travelled from house to house offering to cut silhouettes as a swift and cheap alternative to miniature paintings. Some silhouettes are just portrait profiles but others show figures playing a musical instrument or dancing, while larger more intricate ones may include a family group.

With their stark black profiles outlined against a white background, silhouettes have a sharp impact, their simplicity making as positive a contribution to a modern setting as to more traditional surroundings. They may be displayed in a variety of ways: they can be mounted and framed, pasted directly to the wall in the manner of a print room, or used to decorate screens. Silhouettes are intended to be a spontaneous expression of artistry, but unless you happen to be skilled at cutting them, you will have to resort to other stratagems to make your own. There are various means of doing this, all of which produce convincing results.

The simplest method is to photocopy an existing silhouette. This results in a good sharp image which can be cut out and mounted, or pasted directly to the wall or object to be decorated. A layer of varnish will protect the wall and help achieve an authentic brown-tinged patina of age.

There are books of silhouettes which contain examples of designs from many different periods and countries. As well as eighteenth- and nineteenth-century portraits in the traditional manner, they are likely to include animals, birds, country scenes, conversation pieces – all of which can be cut directly from the page or, if you want to preserve them in the book, photocopied.

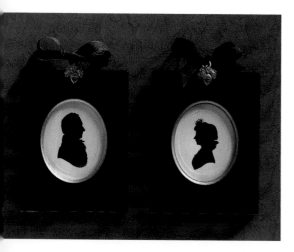

ABOVE *The sharp black and white contrast of silhouettes makes an arresting decorative image. They are traditionally hung in small black lacquer frames but there are numerous other attractive ways in which they can be displayed.*

RIGHT *Original silhouettes can often be found in antique shops. They may, however, be expensive. Much cheaper alternatives are available in specially produced design sourcebooks in which hundreds of silhouettes are printed. They may also be found in less obvious places – Mozart's silhouette on a concert programme, for example. Copies can be made by photocopying or by tracing the images and cutting them out in a good quality matt black paper. It is also possible to make your own silhouettes of family or friends, following the instructions on page 155.*

LEFT *In this family group of silhouettes, the single figures are authentic and still in their original frames, while the large group in the centre is copied from one made in about 1800. It depicts a distant relation of the author with her nine children engaged in various recreational activities.*

BELOW *Elegant and eyecatching, the silhouettes on the top screen are conventionally framed and hung as if they were on the wall.*
Eighteenth-century silhouettes have been photocopied and pasted directly to the surface of the lower screen.

If the silhouettes are to be framed and subjected to close scrutiny, you may prefer to cut them from a matt black paper in the traditional way, first having traced round them from an original. This is not difficult to do. Simply draw round the outline with a soft pencil, then go over this outline on the back of the tracing paper. Place the tracing on the black paper and draw over the original line so that the soft pencil outline is transferred; then carefully cut the silhouette.

You need not be limited to copying silhouettes from sourcebooks. With a little practice you can create a far more individual and personal version, using profiles of your family or friends. All you need do is sit the subject in front of a blank wall to which you have attached a large sheet of drawing paper, then shine a strong light that throws the profile into sharp relief on the wall. Carefully draw round the outline. Reduce the outline on a photocopier to the required size and paint it in with black Indian ink, or transfer the silhouette to black paper by the tracing method described above. An alternative method is to take a photograph of the person in profile. When it is printed, enlarge it, if necessary, on a photocopier to the size that you want, carefully cut round the profile, place it on a sheet of black cartridge paper and draw round it. Cut the silhouette out and mount it on white cartridge paper.

PAPER & LIGHT

When we admire a wallpaper it is the design that captivates us, the paper it is printed on is just a vehicle for the expression of a visual idea. Like a painter's blank canvas, it is an essential tool rather than a material to be appreciated in its own right. Yet paper has a validity of its own, with unique qualities that can be exploited in interiors.

There is a wide range of distinctive papers: cartridge, tissue, crepe, card, tracing – all of which have characteristic surfaces, weights and densities. Paper may be smooth, opaque and highly polished like good writing paper, or tissue thin and transparent like the sheets used to interleave fine art books. Of all its intrinsic qualities, among the most exciting from the decorator's point of view is paper's translucency. Light, whether natural or artificial, shining through paper blinds, screens or lampshades is softened and diffused. Some special hand-made papers incorporating such decorative elements as wild grasses and seeds can only be appreciated when flooded with light, just as a watermark is only visible with the light behind it.

SCREENS & BLINDS

The subtle alchemy of light interacting with paper is nowhere better exploited than in Japan where its ever-changing qualities are considered a vital component in the design of a room. In the absence of the kind of decorative clutter which entertains the eye in Western interiors, the play of light and shadow through white translucent paper on windows and screens establishes a mood which constantly evolves.

While the Japanese approach to interior design may seem a long way removed from the more highly decorated and furnished interiors of the West, the principle of using light filtered through paper to establish an atmosphere of gentle quietness can be adapted with surprising success. A fine white paper blind offers a crisp and stylish alternative to the net or sheer curtains often used either to soften a harsh or glaring light or to ensure privacy. If your windows look out over an unprepossessing cityscape or onto the interior wall of an apartment block, a paper blind that obscures the view is a practical and attractive choice.

Simple bamboo and paper blinds that fold up concertina-style or pull up into a roll have long been popular, and inexpensive, window coverings. If, however, you want to make your own blind, you can do so with a conventional roller blind kit. Instead of fabric, choose a strong paper with an interesting texture that will be revealed as the light shines through it. A plain white blind or screen at the window imposes no particular style: it can either play an active role, perhaps complementing, in its stark plainness, the more minimal requirements of a high-tech modernism or it can blend unobtrusively into the background, flattering rooms that are more traditionally furnished.

LEFT *The quality of light is a remarkable feature of this sparse interior decorated in the Japanese style. Paper-covered screens slide across the windows like shutters, softening and diffusing the light inside. Dappled sunlight shining through the trees casts dancing reflections over the screens, creating constantly changing patterns within the room.*

Screens like this also offer privacy, shutting out the world outside. In spite of its Oriental appearance, this apartment is in fact in central London.

BELOW *Paper screens are used to cut down the glare of brilliant summer sun, creating a cool and tranquil atmosphere in a San Diego apartment.*

LAMPSHADES

Artificial light diffused through white or coloured paper can be equally as captivating as natural light. There is an enormous range of paper shades from which to choose: some exploit the beauty of patterned papers, some have applied decoration, some are pleated, some are pierced to allow shafts of bright light to glimmer through.

Colours only hinted at in curtains, wallpaper and upholstery can be picked up in lampshades, adding the finishing touch to the design scheme. Alternatively, lampshades can introduce an element of surprise: perhaps the one splash of brilliance in an otherwise muted setting. But all the colours in the room will look different by artificial light, and the change is emphasized if the light is glowing through a coloured shade. Everyone knows that soft reds, corals, yellows and terracottas cast a warm, flattering glow, while blues and greens give a cooler light. When choosing a paper shade in any of these colours consider the effect they may have on the colour of the walls and furnishings.

Plain paper shades can be bought quite cheaply and decorated in a variety of ways. Several of the techniques described elsewhere can be applied on a reduced scale: small prints can be pasted to a large card shade to create a miniature print-room effect; or you can use silhouettes (page 154) or other small-scale motifs (page 153) to make a simple collage, perhaps on a particular theme.

Patterns on papers and applied paper motifs can be given a three-dimensional effect by partially cutting around the edge of the design with a sharp knife or scalpel. This should be done carefully, in order to avoid cutting away any areas completely. The cut edges can then be slightly raised, allowing the light to sparkle through and revealing the pattern in an attractive relief of light and shadow. This kind of treatment works particularly well with applied motifs of flowers or foliage.

An intriguing twinkling effect can be achieved by pricking out a design with a pin. Draw the outline motif first in soft pencil, then move along it, pricking through the paper at regular intervals. When you have finished, rub out the pencil line and you will be left with a flowing freehand tracery of tiny glistening lights. If the shade is large enough for your hand to fit into it, the pricks can be made from inside, so that the paper, when pushed through, creates a textured effect on the surface.

It is possible to make your own paper lampshade, using either a strong paper or thin card. Wallpaper or any thin patterned paper, such as an Italian marbled paper, is also suitable, but needs to be strengthened by backing it first with thin card. Whatever you choose, hold the paper against an artificial light before you begin in order to make sure you like the effect it creates.

A small classic shade suitable for a low-wattage candle-bulb can be made from the template printed on this page. Trace round the outline and then transfer the shape to the card or paper you have chosen. (If you wish to make a larger shade, the shape can be scaled up on squared paper or enlarged on a photocopying machine.) On a small shade the edges can look very pretty if they are cut in scallops. Add any further decoration before joining the ends together with double-sided adhesive tape; then mount the finished shade on a small wire lampshade frame.

Pretty but inexpensive, these paper lampshades look as good by day as they do by night. It is easy to make your own shades from good quality card, and to embellish them with applied motifs, cut and pricked designs, pleats, or scalloped edges.

Attractive glimmers of light escape through the cut and pricked floral design on the terracotta shade (top row). The leaves of the trailing wisteria on the large shade (right) are partially cut around so that a brighter light shines through at the edges, throwing them into decorative relief.

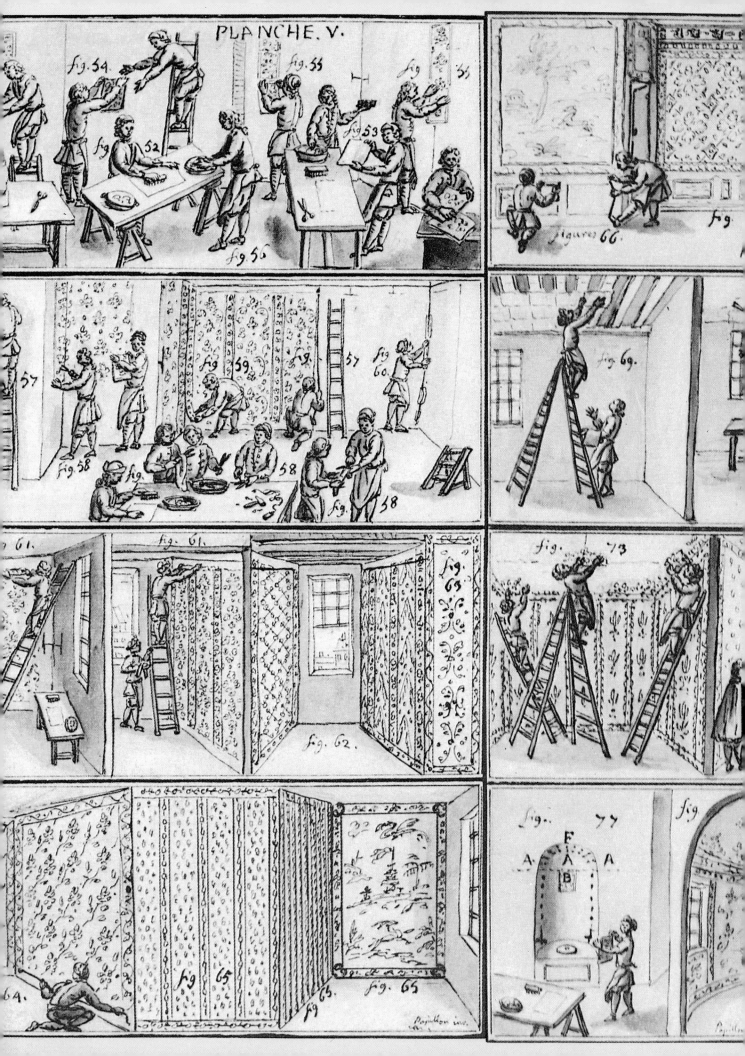

PLANCHE. V.

TECHNIQUES

EQUIPMENT & MATERIALS

Having the right tools for the job is essential for successful paperhanging and makes all the difference between a professional finish and less-than-perfect results. The correct equipment is not expensive and is readily available from any good do-it-yourself or hardware shop. If you are using old or borrowed tools, they must be in good condition.

Pasting brush/roller

You can use a wide paintbrush for pasting, but a special pasting brush, with more flexible bristles, makes it easier to spread the paste evenly.

In the case of certain highly absorbent papers it is preferable to apply the paste directly to the wall, rather than to the paper. If this is necessary, it will be stated on the label. For this you will need a paint roller and tray for the paste.

Paperhanger's brush

This is a wide brush with thick, soft bristles used for smoothing the paper once it is on the wall. The handle is shaped so that it can be held comfortably and used with light pressure to ease the paper into corners and angles without it tearing.

Professionals use hanging brushes measuring 30–33cm/12–13in in width, but these can be awkward for a beginner to handle; a brush about 23cm/9in wide is about right.

Seam roller

A felt or rubber roller is useful for smoothing down the joins between lengths of paper. A wooden or plastic roller can be used for borders but will make a hard line if used on a wallpaper join.

Wallpaper shears and scissors

A good pair of wallpaper shears will make the paperhanger's job much easier. They are large, with blades about 15cm/6in in length, for making long cuts. The points are specially shaped to crease the paper as it meets an angle, giving a line to cut along.

Do not be tempted to use dressmaking or kitchen scissors as you may get jagged cuts. You will, however, need a small pair of ordinary sharp-pointed scissors for snipping and trimming.

Trimming knife

In some tight corners, a knife is more useful than scissors. It can also be used to cut long, straight lines with a steel rule. A craft knife with replaceable blades is ideal. Make sure that the blade is very sharp.

Steel rule

Professionals use a long metal metre rule or yardstick and a trimming knife for cutting straight lines down the length of the wallpaper. An ordinary short ruler is much harder to manage and usually results in wavy lines. You will also need a short metal ruler and a retractable steel tape measure.

Plumb line and chalk

A plumb line consists of a string with a weight attached. It is used to mark vertical lines on the wall so that the paper can be positioned to hang absolutely straight. You can either buy a plumb line or make one with some non-stretch string and a small, flat heavy object. You will also need some chalk or charcoal to rub into the string in order to mark the vertical on the wall.

Spirit level

A spirit level can be placed either horizontally or vertically alongside a border or pencilled guideline to check that it is straight. If it is, the air bubble appears exactly in the centre of the glass tube.

Pasting table

Any reasonably long table is suitable for pasting, as long as its surface will not be damaged by paste or water. However, purpose-built tables are cheap, lightweight, and can be folded away when not in use. They are also narrower than conventional tables – and this makes pasting easier.

Stepladder

A stable stepladder is vital for paperhanging; balancing on a chair or a stool is not safe and rather difficult. An aluminium stepladder is lightweight and easy to move around, and one with a platform as the top step is useful for holding equipment.

If you are papering a ceiling, you will need an extra stepladder and a wooden plank or a multipurpose ladder.

Adhesive

Different kinds of wallpaper require different kinds of paste. Buy the paper first, and follow the manufacturer's recommendations regarding paste; this is vital for a successful result.

Size

A coating of size (generally a dilution of the wallpaper paste) is necessary to prevent the adhesive from soaking into the walls and producing dry spots under the wallpaper. It also facilitates repositioning the paper on the wall. Size can be applied with an ordinary paintbrush or with a pasting brush.

The label on the paper will specify which kind of size to use.

Buckets, sponge, cloths

You will need two buckets, one for the paste and another, larger one for water. You will also need a soft cellulose sponge to wipe off any paste that gets onto the wallpaper surface. This is more suitable than a cloth and can be quickly rinsed in clean water if it becomes sticky.

You will also need plenty of soft clean cloths, for more general cleaning up, and some old sheets for protecting floor and furniture.

Various other tools and materials may be required for preparing the wall surface. These might include glasspaper, a filling compound for cracks and holes, a filling knife, a scraper and wire brush for removing old wallpaper, a steam stripper, primer and sealer. These items are described in greater detail in the section on 'Preparing walls' on page 164.

ESTIMATING QUANTITIES

There are several variables to consider when calculating the amount of wallpaper you will need: the dimensions of the room, the width and length per roll of the paper you have chosen (both of which vary according to the manufacturer and the country of origin), and the length of the pattern repeat. Your interior design or decorating shop will certainly advise on quantities but will need accurate measurements of the room in order to give a correct estimate.

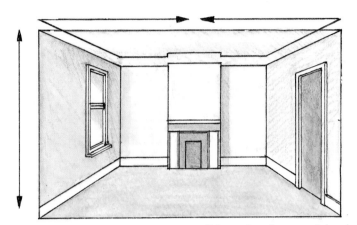

Measuring the room

1 First measure around the entire room, including doors and windows, alcoves and chimney breasts.

Then measure the height of the room from the ceiling or base of the cornice down to the skirting board. Measure between picture rail and/or dado rail if you are confining the paper to this area.

2 If the paper is plain or has a pattern that does not require matching, add 10cm/4in to the height measurement for trimming – 5cm/2in at both top and bottom. This gives the length of a drop, or full length of paper.

If the paper has a pattern repeat, each length will have to be hung at the same level, but the entire length of the repeat (as well as the 10cm/4in) must be added to each drop, in order that you can position the pattern correctly.

Some wallpapers with very large repeats should be hung using alternate rolls, which will minimize wastage. In the sample book you will find precise instructions on allowing for the repeat.

Calculating the amount to buy

1 Once you have chosen the paper, divide the total distance around the room (obtained in step **1** of 'Measuring the room') by the width of the paper. This gives the number of drops you will need.

2 Now divide the length of the roll by the length of a drop (again, see step **1** 'Measuring the room') to get the number of drops that can be cut from each roll.

It is safest to include fireplaces, windows and doors in these calculations, even though this will entail some wastage. However, if you are intending to use an expensive paper ask the shop assistant to adjust the number of drops to allow for these openings.

3 Finally, divide the total number of drops required by the number of drops per roll; this is the number of rolls you need to buy. It is a good idea to add a roll to this total to allow for mistakes in cutting or for spoiling a length when hanging. Buy all the rolls at the outset, making sure that they are from the same printing batch; the number is printed on the label. Colours vary, if only slightly, from one batch to another, and variations will show up on the wall. If you have underestimated and need more rolls, quote the batch number when re-ordering and check the rolls on delivery to make sure that they are from the same batch.

PREPARING WALLS FOR PAPERING

The quality of the finished result depends on the condition of the wall surface beneath the paper. So do not be tempted to neglect the preparation in your eagerness to get on with the creative part of the job, for you will certainly regret it later.

The amount of preparation required varies according to the paper chosen. With a textured paper or a lively print, slight irregularities will probably not be visible, whereas with a subtle stripe or a plain paper they may be glaringly evident. If in doubt, err on the side of caution.

Before starting work, remove as much furniture as you can. Move any remaining furniture to the centre of the room and cover it and the floor with dust sheets.

Papering over paint

A wall that has previously been painted and is in good condition will only need to be washed. Do this with sugar soap and a sponge.

If the paint is gloss, rub it over slightly with glasspaper to provide a key for the paste. (Wrap the glasspaper over a wooden block to make it easier to handle.) Then wash the wall to remove the dust.

If the wall has been painted with distemper or whitewash, wash it off thoroughly, otherwise it will prevent the wallpaper from sticking properly.

Removing old wallpaper

In most cases it is advisable to remove old wallpaper before applying new. The original paper may be on the verge of coming loose, and a new layer would hasten the process. New paper should never be applied over metallic, flocked, washable or vinyl papers. However, vinyl papers are made of two layers, the top one of which can be carefully peeled away, leaving a useful lining paper.

For removing old paper, the basic equipment is a scraper (a knife resembling a filling knife but with a stiff blade), a wire brush, a bucket of warm water and a sponge.

1 Score the surface of the paper with the wire brush. (Some scrapers have a serrated edge which can be used for this.) This helps the water penetrate the surface and soften the paste.

2 Soak the wall thoroughly with warm water; a few drops of vinegar or liquid detergent added to the water will help the soaking process.

3 Use the scraper to remove the paper, taking care not to dig in to the plaster (**a**). Re-soak the walls as necessary.

If the wallpaper resists ordinary soaking, you may succeed in loosening it with a proprietary chemical stripper. Choose one intended for wallpaper, not paint, and follow the manufacturer's instructions when using it.

In very stubborn cases, or if you want to do the job speedily, use a steam wallpaper stripper. You can hire one inexpensively from a do-it-yourself shop. Simply apply the steam pad directly to the wall with one hand while scraping the previously softened adjacent area with the other (**b**). The steamer will speed up the process; however, there is some risk of loosening the plaster, and you may prefer to get professional help with this job.

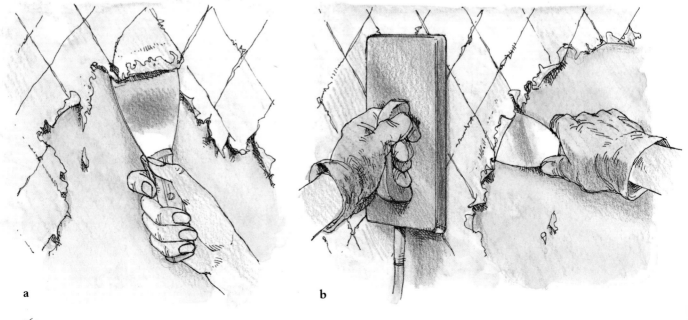

a   b

c   d

Repairing holes and cracks

For this you will need a resin-based filling compound, available in both ready-mixed and powder form, and a filling knife with a wide, flexible, squared-off blade.

1 First remove any loose plaster. If you are filling a crack, undercut it first to provide a secure grip for the filling (**c**). Using a scraper, cut into the crack diagonally to form a V shape with the widest part of the V inside. Brush out all loose plaster.

2 Apply the filler with the filling knife, pressing the blade flat over the hole (**d**). Make sure that no air is trapped under the filler.

3 When the hole or crack is filled, scrape the knife across the top, to remove the excess and make the surface as smooth as possible.

If a hole is large, fill it in stages, applying the filler in layers about 3mm/⅛in thick and allowing each to dry before adding the next one.

4 When the filler has dried, rub the surface down with glasspaper.

Undecorated walls

Allow newly plastered walls to dry out for several months. Then give them a coat of primer or sealer before papering them. Treat cement walls with a masonry sealer.

Sizing the wall surface

Once the wall surface is smooth and clean, size it to prevent it from absorbing the paste too quickly, which would make it difficult to re-position the paper when hanging. The manufacturer will recommend a suitable size for the type of wallpaper. Usually it is simply a weak solution of the paste to be used with the paper.

Apply the size with the pasting brush, or with a large paintbrush, as evenly as possible. Make sure that it is thoroughly dry before papering.

LINING WALLS

Some people think that a lining paper is unnecessary, but if you want to get a completely smooth and professional finish it is essential. Because it is neutral in colour, lining paper is especially useful when applying a light-coloured wallpaper over a wall that has previously been painted a dark colour. It also gives you the chance to practise hanging paper and to solve the problems of a particular room before attempting the final papering. Lining paper comes in several weights; a medium-weight paper is suitable for most purposes. With it you should use the size and adhesive recommended for the top paper.

Hanging lining paper

Professional decorators hang lining paper horizontally (called cross-lining) which prevents any possibility of the seams of the two layers coinciding. However, this is a tricky manoeuvre, and the inexperienced paperhanger should hang the lining paper vertically, following the instructions given below for hanging the top paper. (If you do wish to cross-line, follow the instructions for hanging horizontally on page 179.)

Begin at the point chosen for the first drop (see page 166), but hang the first drop of lining paper slightly to the left or the right of this position (**e**). In this way, the joins will be staggered. At corners, trim the paper and butt the edges together (rather than overlapping them, as when hanging top paper at corners). Allow the lining to dry before hanging the top paper.

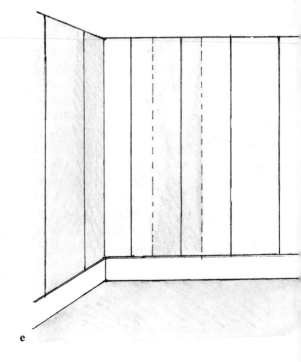

e

PAPERING WALLS

If you are intending to paper both walls and ceiling, tackle the ceiling first. Instructions for papering ceilings are given on pages 174–175.

Before beginning to hang the wallpaper you should plan positioning carefully. The first length should be positioned at the focal point of the room. This might be above the fireplace, the wall between two windows or the centre of the most important wall. Start in the middle of this wall and work out to either side.

If the paper is patterned, decide on the place where it will meet; since the pattern is unlikely to match precisely it should be an inconspicuous place such as an inner corner near a door.

Plain wallpapers are much easier to hang than patterned ones because there is no design to match. A small, regular pattern will present few problems, but a large pattern repeat requires care in cutting the first drop to make sure that the design looks balanced on the wall. Hold the first length against the wall before cutting to determine the ideal position and also to make sure that it is the right way up (even professionals have been known to hang paper upside down!). Hang a complete motif at the top, rather than cutting it through the middle.

a

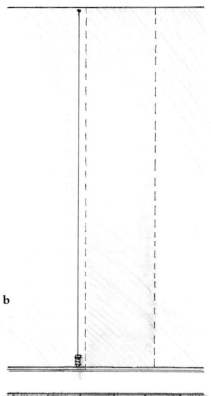

b

Cutting the lengths

Cut a number of drops – enough for one wall, or perhaps for the whole room – and then paste and hang a few of these at a time.

1 Measure and cut the first drop, allowing 10cm/4in extra for trimming (5cm/2in at both top and bottom).

2 Cut the following drops, holding each one next to the previous one as shown and adjusting it to match the pattern before cutting (**a**). (Papers with little or no pattern can simply be placed on top of the first drop and cut to the same length.)

If the paper has a large repeat, cut the lengths from two different rolls, alternately, following the manufacturer's instructions, to minimize wastage.

Cut the lengths on the pasting table, first having made sure that there is no paste on it. As a precaution you might cover the table with a length of lining paper and move this along or replace it if you get paste on it.

If you are matching a large pattern, you may find it more comfortable to cut on the floor, rather than on the narrow pasting table.

Finding the true vertical

Before you hang the first drop, you must mark a true vertical line on the wall. Do not rely on windows or doors being straight or even parallel to each other; if you do, the result is likely to be vertical slant all the way around the room. Use a plumb line to mark the wall where one edge of the paper will be placed.

1 Find the centre point for the first strip, then measure off to one side half the width of the paper. Mark this point at the top of the wall.

2 Measure off a length of string the distance from the ceiling or cornice to the skirting board. Rub chalk into the string (or charcoal, if the surface is light). Tie one end to the weight, and fasten the other with a nail to the mark at the top of the wall (**b**).

3 When the plumb line is hanging still, hold the weight firmly against the skirting board and flick the string so it rebounds against the wall. This will mark a vertical line.

Pasting the paper

1 Lay the paper face down on the pasting table, with one edge overlapping the table slightly and the lower end hanging off the end of the table. Secure it at the upper end with the shears or another heavy object to prevent it from rolling up.

2 Starting at the upper end, apply a line of paste down the centre of the paper, then paste out to the overlapping edge, covering the paper evenly with criss-crossing diagonal strokes (**c**). Apply the paste generously; difficulties in hanging paper, such as air bubbles, often arise from having used too little paste. Take care to avoid lumps.

3 Slide the paper so that the unpasted edge slightly overlaps the table, and paste to the edge in the same way. Make sure that the edges are well covered with paste.

4 Fold the pasted end over so that it lies somewhat past the middle of the drop, then slide the unpasted end up onto the table. Paste this end in the same way, and fold it to meet the other end. The shorter fold at the lower end makes it easy to distinguish top from bottom (**d**).

5 Lay the folded paper on the floor, and allow the paste to soak into it for a few minutes so that it becomes pliable; follow the manufacturer's recommendations for the time. This is important because too little soaking may result in bubbles. Too much, and the paste will dry before you have got it on the wall. When the paper is ready for hanging, lift it as shown (**e**).

Ready-pasted papers

Ready-pasted papers are supplied along with a tray, or trough, for wetting. Cut the paper into lengths as for an unpasted paper. Partially fill the tray with water, and place it next to the wall where the strip is to be hung; roll up the paper loosely, with the top edge on the outside, and immerse it in the tray for the length of time specified by the manufacturer. Then gently unroll the paper (**f**) and apply it to the wall as described on page 168.

167

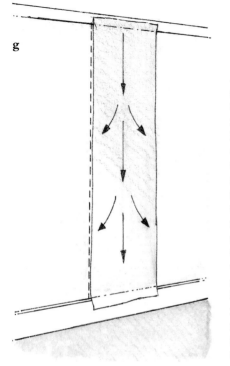

g

To hang the paper

1 Unfold the top end of the paper and place it against the wall, holding the upper edge approximately 5cm/ 2in above the top of the wall and lining the vertical edge up to the chalked vertical line. Make sure that the paper falls straight down the chalk line, adjusting it if necessary. If the positioning is incorrect, gently lift the paper from the bottom and readjust it. Use the hanging brush to smooth the paper very lightly down the middle and out towards the sides, working downwards (**g**), and removing any large air bubbles by lifting and repositioning it. (When the paper is still damp small bubbles may be noticeable; but do not be alarmed, they will disappear as it dries.)

2 To finish the top edge, push the tips of the wallpaper shears against the ceiling line to crease the paper slightly (**h**). Peel the paper gently back and cut evenly along the fold line (**i**). Then brush the paper back into place. Repeat the process at the lower edge. The edges can be pressed down gently with a felt roller, but avoid too much pressure, which will cause a line or indentation. Wipe off any excess paste from the ceiling, skirting board or paper.

3 To hang the second length, cut and paste as described above. Line it up against the first strip with the edges butted together, not overlapping. Continue in this way until you reach a corner, where a different technique (see below) is required.

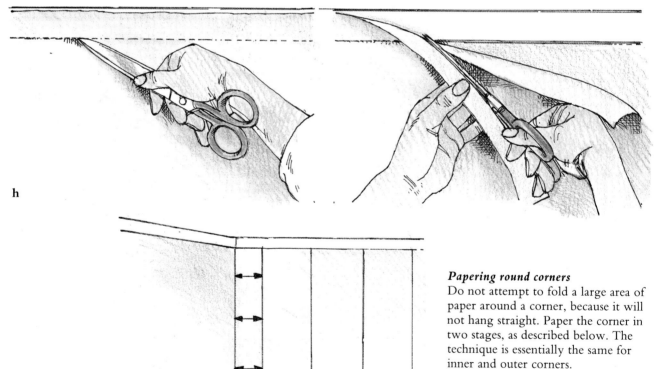

h

j

Papering round corners

Do not attempt to fold a large area of paper around a corner, because it will not hang straight. Paper the corner in two stages, as described below. The technique is essentially the same for inner and outer corners.

1 When the last full width near a corner has been pasted, measure the remaining distance. Measure at several points down the wall (**j**), because the distance may vary. Take the greatest distance and add 5mm/ $\frac{1}{4}$in to it. This is the required width of the drop.

2 Mark this width on the paper and cut, using the steel rule as a guide for a perfectly straight line.

3 Paste and hang the partial width in the usual way, taking the extra 5mm/¼in around the corner. On an inner corner, brush it firmly into the corner using the tips of the bristles. If the wall is uneven, make tiny snips in the turned edge so that it will lie smoothly (**k**).

4 Measure from the corner a distance equal to the width of the paper left over when you cut the previous drop, plus 5mm/¼in, and mark a vertical at this point with a plumb line.

5 Cut a drop to this width. The cut edge will overlap the previously pasted drop by about 5mm/¼in. The outer edge is pasted to align with the new vertical (**l**).

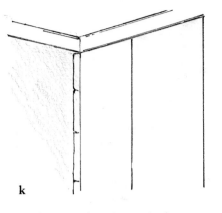

k

If you are hanging a vinyl paper you will need to use a latex adhesive where the edges overlap. Roll the edge firmly with a seam roller to ensure a secure join.

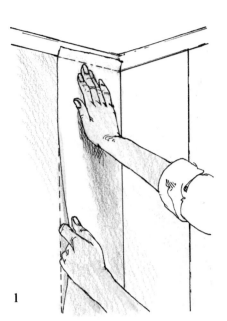

l

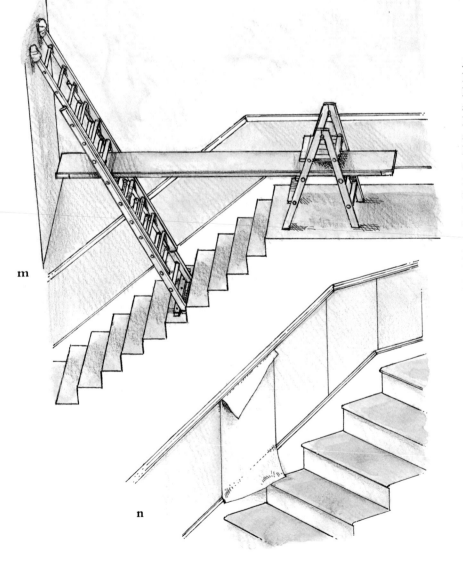

m

n

Hanging paper along stairs

Papering a stairwell, or even a single long flight of stairs is really a job for a professional. It requires at least two ladders, plus one or more platforms all rigged together securely. The ladders must be fixed to the floor and/or stair treads (with the carpet first removed) by means of battens nailed securely in place (**m**). Needless to say, a good head for heights is also essential.

It is relatively easy, however, to paper alongside a short flight of steps, where the ladder can simply be placed at the top of the steps and then at the bottom. In this case, the only special technique is trimming the lower edge at an angle.

Cut the paper to measure the distance to the lowest point of the slope, adding the usual allowances (see page 163) for trimming and pattern matching. Then, after positioning the drop, press the blades of the scissors into the groove at the skirting, pull the paper away, and trim along the crease. Press the trimmed paper into place.

Essentially the same technique is used at the upper edge if you are hanging a dado along stairs. In this case the paper is creased along the lower edge of the dado rail (**n**).

DOORS AND WINDOWS

Papering around doors and windows requires different techniques, depending on the surrounding structure and moulding.

Non-recessed doors and windows

1 Hang the first overlapping length untrimmed (**a**).

2 Cut around the frame, leaving an overlap of about 5cm/2in. Press the paper against the frame to mark the corner. Cut diagonally into the corner (**b**).

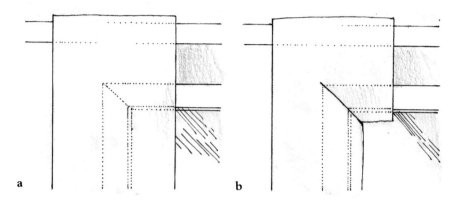

a   b

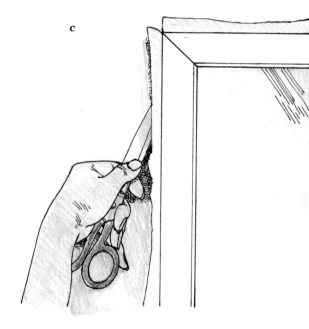

c

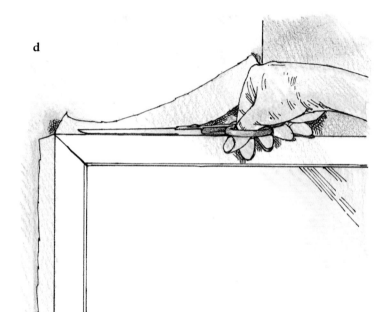

d

3 Press the paper into position, creasing it firmly with the shears (**c**), and trim as usual, being careful not to tear the paper at the corner (**d**).

4 At the lower edge of a window frame the procedure is basically the same as at the top, although a projecting sill requires a slightly different technique at the corners. Let the paper hang over the windowsill, then cut horizontally through the paper. Snip the edges (**e**), taking care not to cut too deeply, push the paper into the angle (**f**) and trim.

5 Hang short lengths above and below the frame in the usual way, then hang the next full drop as described in steps *1–3* above.

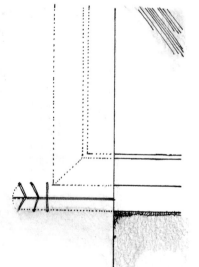

e   f

Shallow recessed windows

If the window is set in from the wall by only a small amount – 3cm/1in or so – you can just turn the paper round the edge of the wall. First trim it to measure slightly more than the required amount, then press it into the edge of the window frame, crease and trim to fit.

If the reveal is deeper – up to 20cm/8in – you can take the side edge round the corner as shown below.

1 When you hang the full drop along the side edge of the reveal, do not stick it down firmly. Cut along the upper edge of the recess and the sill (**g**).

2 Cut a piece to fit into the top of the reveal at the corner (**h**). This should measure the depth of the reveal (A–B) plus 3cm/1in for turning up at the front; in width it should be the distance from the corner of the reveal to the edge of the wallpaper above (C–D) (so that the seams will be

aligned) plus about 3cm/1in to turn down at the corner.

3 Gently peeling back the full drop, paste this piece into the upper corner of the reveal (**i**), taking care to align its edge with that of the upper piece; press the other edge into the corner.

4 Paste the free vertical edge of the main strip to the side of the reveal. Short drops above the window should be cut long enough to also cover the top of the reveal (**j**).

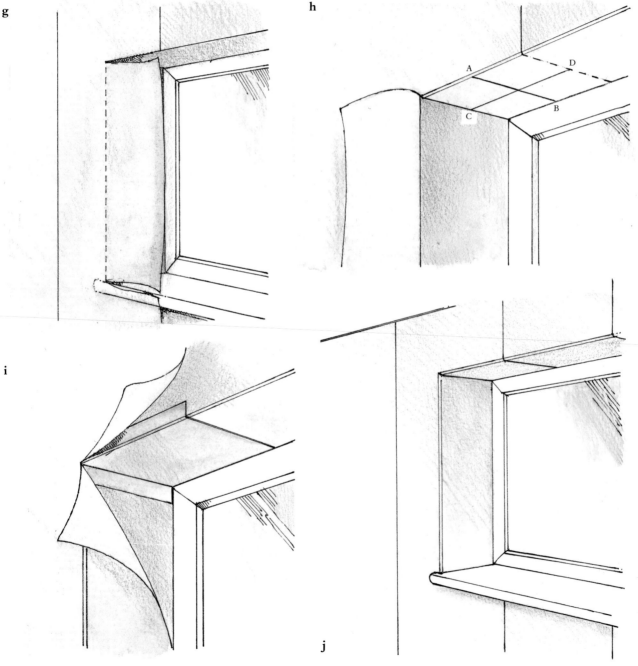

g

h

i

j

Deeply recessed or bay windows

If you wish to paper the ceiling as well as the sides of a deeply recessed window with a paper that has a noticeable pattern, it is possible to get a perfect match by following the hanging sequence suggested in the sketch (**k**). If your paper is plain or has a tiny repeating motif the hanging sequence is not so crucial.

If the wallpaper happens to end with a complete drop at the edge of the recess, it is quite simple to paper the ceiling and walls in the sequence shown, so that the joins fall in the same position.

However, this recommended order, while explaining the principle behind achieving a successful match, is only a guide. The individual window and the position in which the seams fall on the main wall may dictate a slightly different order of hanging.

Archway

Paper the wall first, then the inside of the arch.

1 After papering the wall, trim the excess to about 3cm/1in or so. Snip into the excess to ease it round the curve and turn the edges to the underside of the arch. Cut off any tiny overlapping bits to make the surface as smooth as possible (**l**).

Repeat on the other side of the arch, if necessary.

2 Cut the strip for the inner arch to the exact width of the arch. If the paper has a noticeable vertical repeat, cut two strips, each slightly longer than the height, to be joined at the centre.

3 Fold the strip concertina-like and paste it in place (**m**). If you are using two strips, overlap their upper edges at the centre, cut through both strips with a knife, remove the offcuts and butt the trimmed ends together.

For an arched recess the process is similar, but before hanging the strip(s) on the arch, paper the inner wall area. If the arch has a steep slope, like a Gothic arch, the paper may be trimmed slightly to shape to make it easier to fit the apex of the arch. But beware of cutting away too much. Snip the paper edges and paste them to the inside of the arch. Make sure to align the seams and the pattern repeat.

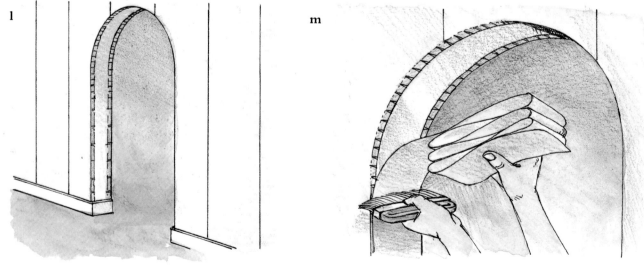

n

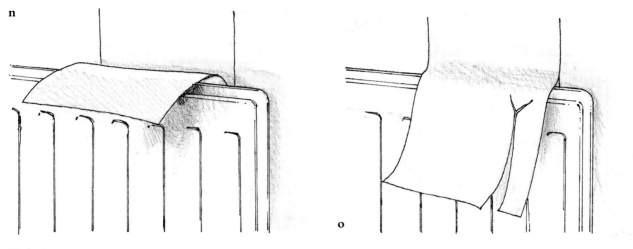

o

Radiators
1 Cut and paste a full drop of paper, but only smooth the top half onto the wall. Press the lower end down onto the top brackets holding the radiator to the wall (**n**).
2 Pull the paper out, then cut upwards from the lower edge to the creases marking the bracket positions, making a V shape at the top (**o**).
3 Smooth the lower end down behind the radiator, using a cloth wrapped around a stick.

p

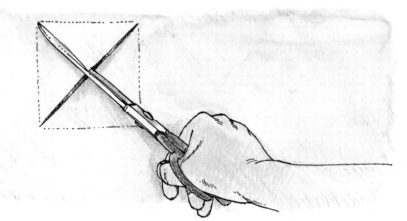

q

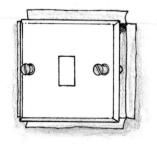

r

Electric sockets and light switches
First turn off the electricity.
1 Hang the paper and smooth it gently over the switch or socket plate to reveal the outline.
2 Cut diagonally from the centre of the shape almost to each corner (**p**) and peel the paper back.
3 If possible, loosen the screws holding the switch plate, trim the paper edges to within about 1cm/½in of the plate edge (**q**) and slip them under the plate. Tighten the screws. (*Important: do not use this method with foil papers, which conduct electricity.*)

Alternatively, simply crease the edges of the flaps closely around the switch or socket plate and trim them with a knife (**r**).

Rehanging pictures
If you want to rehang pictures or bookshelf brackets in the same position as before, mark their positions with matchsticks. Insert the matchsticks in the holes, then break them off close to the wall surface. Press the paper gently over the matchsticks so that it is pierced neatly.

PAPERING CEILINGS

Although there are fewer obstructions to deal with, papering a ceiling is considerably more difficult than papering a wall – simply in terms of the physical effort – and is best not attempted by the novice. If you do need to paper a ceiling, enlist a helper, and take special care to set up a secure working platform.

You will need either two stepladders and a plank or special decorators' trestles, which can be hired from some do-it-yourself shops. Prepare the ceiling as described for walls, pages 164–165.

The ceiling should be papered before the walls, and the paper should be hung parallel to a wall containing a window, beginning at that wall and working away from it.

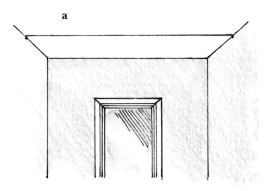

1 Measure inwards along the ceiling from the starting wall, and mark off a distance about 3cm/1in less than the width of the roll of paper at both sides of the ceiling. Rub chalk or charcoal into a piece of string and fasten the string to the ceiling at both points (**a**). Snap the string to mark a line on the ceiling.

2 Remove the string and measure along the line. Cut the first strip to this measurement plus about 10cm/4in. Cut the remaining strips, adding extra for matching the pattern, if any, and adjusting the length for any wider parts of the room.

3 Paste each length as described on page 167, but fold it concertina-style to make it easy to handle (**b**).

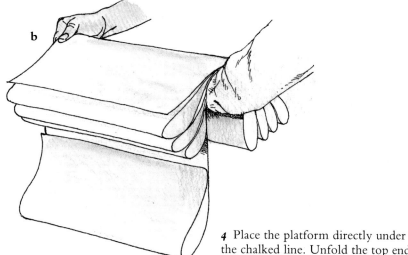

4 Place the platform directly under the chalked line. Unfold the top end of the paper and smooth it in place along the chalked line, supporting the folds with a cardboard tube. Gently press the excess into the angle with the wall, using the paperhanger's brush. Move along the platform, unfolding the paper and smoothing it in place. Make sure you keep the inner edge aligned with the chalked line (**c**).

5 Cut into the corners to enable the excess paper to lie flat. Press the edges firmly into the angle, using shears (**d**). Pull the ends away from the wall, and trim them to about 1cm/½in. Brush the paper back into place. If the walls are not to be papered, trim the edges precisely at the angle of wall and ceiling.

6 Without moving the platform, hang the next length of paper, butting its edge to the previously pasted edge. When hanging subsequent lengths, move the platform directly under the edge of the previously pasted length.

Papering round ceiling roses
First turn off the electricity at the mains and remove the shade and bulb.
1 Paper up to the rose and press the paper against the flex outlet to mark the central point. Cut a cross at this point large enough to slip the lampholder and flex through.
2 Enlarge the cross, cutting it in triangular flaps so that the rose cover will slip through it. Unscrew the rose cover then trim the flaps of paper back (**e**). Screw the rose cover back in place.

When papering round the corner of an alcove or recess cut the paper diagonally (**f**, **g**), and trim away the excess.

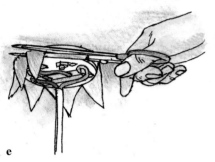

e

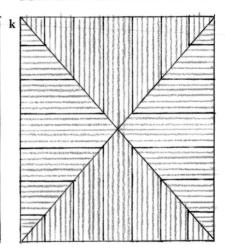

f

g

Mitred striped ceiling
A mitred striped ceiling is less difficult to paper than it may appear. Since the ceiling is divided into four sections, the drops of paper are shorter than normal and therefore relatively easy to handle.
1 Using string rubbed with chalk or charcoal (see page 166), mark diagonal lines on the ceiling (**h**).
2 Having thus located the mid-point of the ceiling, measure the length of each wall and mark the halfway point. Mark chalked lines joining these points to the centre point. The central stripe of the wallpaper must run down these lines.
3 If the centre stripe of the paper corresponds with the centre of the roll, as is normally the case, measure off half the width of the wallpaper to one side and mark another chalk line straight across the ceiling to indicate the edge of the first strip of paper.

Mark a similar guideline at right angles to this one (**i**).

If your stripe design is not centred on the roll you will have to adjust these guidelines accordingly.
4 Cut the first drop to measure from one wall to the centre point, adding the usual allowance for trimming.
5 Paste the drop to the ceiling, aligning one edge with the straight chalked line, and overlapping the centre point slightly. Smooth it lightly in position, then pull back the edges along the diagonal lines, crease and trim (**j**). Absolute accuracy is not essential, as the edges will be covered with a border. Trim the edge at the wall.

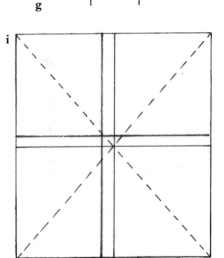

h

i

j

k

6 Apply the adjacent, shorter drops in the same way to fill this first section of the ceiling (**k**).
7 Repeat steps *3–5* in the remaining sections of wall.

BORDERS, DADOS & FRIEZES

Wherever you are hanging a border, it must be straight. Unless you have an existing straight line to work to – a dado or picture rail, for example – you will have to draw a guideline. If you wish to hang a border next to an uneven or sloping ceiling, the irregularity will be less noticeable if you take it from the lowest point of the ceiling, hang it straight and paint the exposed area above the border the same colour as the ceiling.

Measuring quantities

For a simple border along the top of the wall, measure round the entire room. Double this if you are bordering the skirting board, too, but deduct the width of the door(s).

Measure round doors and windows, if they are to be bordered, adding a little extra for mitring corners. Add the height of the room if you intend to border the walls at the sides. Remember to take the border up both walls at the corner. Allow a little extra for errors.

Marking guidelines

These are essential if you are to achieve a professional-looking finish.

Borders at picture rail level

1 Measure down from the ceiling and mark the wall very lightly with a pencil at several points. Using a straight edge as a guide, join these points to indicate the edge of the border.
2 Check with a spirit level that the line is horizontal.

Borders at dado level

1 Measure up from the skirting board at intervals; join the line and check with a spirit level.
2 To hang the border on a diagonal up the stairs, mark a vertical at the top and bottom of the slope, using a plumb line (see page 166). Measure up from the skirting at both points and mark the height of the border.
3 Mark the height of the border at intervals between these points and join the marks using a straight edge. Alternatively, fasten a chalked line between the top and lower points and flick it against the wall to mark a guideline.

Outlining doors and windows

Hang the border up to the edge of the frame. If it appears to be slightly crooked, ease it, while the paste is still damp, closer or farther away from the frame as necessary.

Applying borders

Use a strong ready-mixed tub paste or a special border adhesive.

1 Cut a length of border, making it as long as possible.
2 Cover the pasting table with a sheet of lining paper, which can be changed as necessary. Apply the paste generously using a pasting brush and taking care to paste thoroughly to the edges to prevent peeling. This is especially important with borders that have curved or angled edges. As you paste, fold the border concertina-style (**a**). This makes it easier to handle.
3 Ideally, hang the border from right to left if you are right-handed; from left to right if you are left-handed. Smooth it lightly in place with a cloth as you go along. Then, when you are confident that it is correct, go over it more firmly, taking special care to press down the edges with a seam roller. Wipe excess paste away carefully with a damp sponge (**b**).
4 At a join, overlap the paper slightly unless this spoils the pattern match (**c**). If it does, butt the joins instead, pasting them firmly together so they do not open to leave a gap when dry.

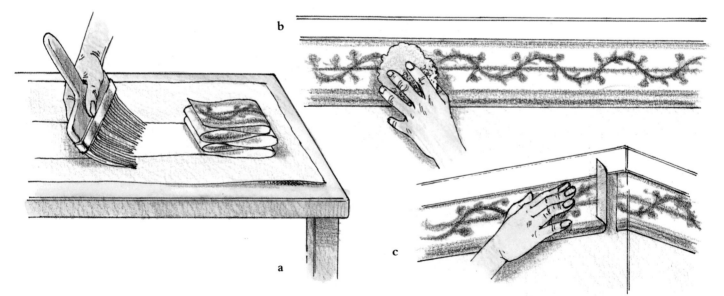

Mitring right-angled corners

Use one of the following methods to mitre the corners of the border as you proceed. Instructions for matching large patterns at corners are given on pages 180–181.

Method 1

1 Paste the vertical border to the wall, leaving the end square and taking it to the outer edge of the border position.

2 Cut the horizontal border slightly longer than required, and paste it to the wall, almost up to the vertical strip. Fold it back so that it makes a 45° angle, matching the pattern on the vertical border (**d**). Crease it sharply along this fold, and cut along the crease.

3 Paste it over the vertical strip (**e**).

The advantage of this method is that even if the cut is slightly inaccurate, or if the border should shrink a little, there is never a gap.

Method 2

1 Cut both borders slightly longer than necessary and paste to the wall lapping one corner over the other. Cut diagonally through both strips (**f**), using a metal straight edge and a knife.

2 Paste the trimmed edges in place (**g**).

This is a simpler method and results in a smooth butt join. The same method is used if you are joining borders at different angles, or if you need to mitre a succession of difficult angles – for example, around a fireplace with a stepped outline.

A slight curve can be followed by snipping the border at regular intervals almost all the way across it and then overlapping the edges (**h**). The pattern will be distorted slightly so bear this in mind when choosing the border.

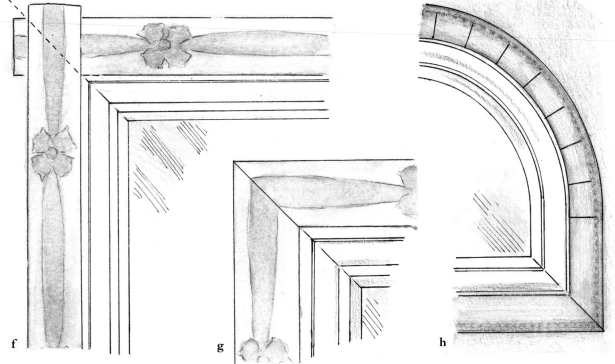

Borders supplied in separate pieces
such as the rope and swagged borders
illustrated on pages 114–115, or the
Gothick arch border shown on
page 2, can be made to fit any wall
length exactly, with the swags always
finishing perfectly in the corners.

1 Measure the length of each wall.
Then measure the length of one
swag. Divide the wall measurement
by this figure to give the number of
swags needed. If there is a small
amount over, use it up by leaving
gaps between the pieces (**a**) to be
covered by rosettes, bows or knots. If
the swags take up slightly more space
than the wall length, overlap the
pieces (**b**) and cover the joins. With
some designs the joins are not
covered, but the amount of overlap is
varied to ensure an exact fit (**c, d**).

2 It is easiest to lay the swags out on
the floor to check the layout, leaving
equal gaps between them or
overlapping them as necessary.

a

b

c

d

e

Alternatively, you can measure the
wall, marking the position of each
element exactly.

3 Repeat this process for the other
walls.

4 Paste the swags (as instructed on
page 176). If appropriate, cover the
gaps or overlaps with rosettes, bows
or knots (**e**).

5 At the corners, fix the rosettes
bows or knots so they are centred on
the wall angle to give a continuous
effect (**f**).

f

Photocopied borders

1 Once you have chosen your border design, enlarge or reduce it if necessary to the required depth (**g**). Make several copies of this size, and paste them to a sheet of A3 paper as shown on page 79. By using larger paper you keep the number of joins to a minimum, and fitting several side by side reduces the cost.

2 Photocopy this page onto good-quality paper – white, if you wish to colour the design later, or tinted paper if you want a duotone effect (**h**). Spray with artist's fixative so that the ink does not smudge. Commercial photocopiers will usually have a range of suitable papers, or will use paper that you provide. It is important to choose one that is reasonably thick, otherwise it may crumple and crease when hung.

3 Cut out the border pieces, using a metal straight edge and knife if the edges are straight, or scissors if they are curved, and paste them to the wall. Join the edges together carefully (**i**) to give a continuous design.

Hanging dados & friezes

A dado is hung just like a full-length drop of paper, except that the upper edge is trimmed to fit snugly under the dado rail. Instructions on hanging dados up staircases are given on page 169. Friezes can be treated as extra-wide borders (see page 176).

To hang a width of wallpaper horizontally to make a dado or frieze, measure and cut the paper to the length of the wall. A length of paper will normally turn around a chimney breast or shallow window without falling out of alignment but do not attempt to take very long lengths of paper round corners. If you need a guideline, follow the method for marking one suggested on page 176.

Paste the paper in the normal way (see page 167), allowing the paste to soak into it until it is pliable. Then fold the paper loosely into a manageable concertina. Starting in a corner, paste down one end and begin to unfold the rest of the strip, smoothing the paper to the wall as you go (**a**). When hanging paper horizontally in a dado, you may need to use more than one width of the paper. Start under the dado rail and work downwards. Cut the second piece about 2.5cm/1in deeper than needed before pasting it. Smooth into position trimming any excess above the skirting board (**b**).

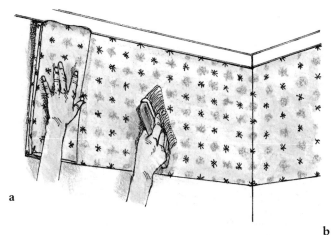

PANELS

It may be helpful to begin by drawing a plan of the walls on squared paper including the position of doors and windows. Start by deciding on the position of the most important panel. This might be in the middle of the main wall or over the fireplace. Then decide on the arrangement of panels either side. The spacing and arrangement of the panels should be adjusted to suit the room. As a general rule, the spacing around the panels should be equal, but you may allow a slightly deeper space between the base of the panel and the skirting board.

If you are making outline panels with borders, draw them to scale and experiment with different proportions. Panels filled with a contrasting paper can be arranged like outline panels or, alternatively, you can make each panel the exact width of your wallpaper and run borders round the edge to form the frame, adjusting the space between panels to fill the wall. It may also be possible to use half the width or a width and a half of the wallpaper to create a complete motif within the panel. This was the method used in the bedroom illustrated on pages 100–101.

Special effects, such as the arrangement shown on page 96, should be planned carefully on the squared-paper plan. If the wallpaper has little or no pattern, cut small pieces of it and move them around on your plan until you are pleased with the arrangement.

b

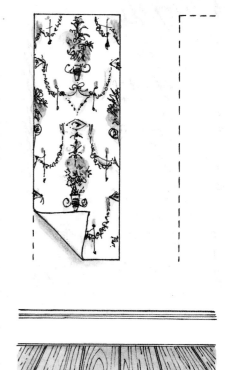

a

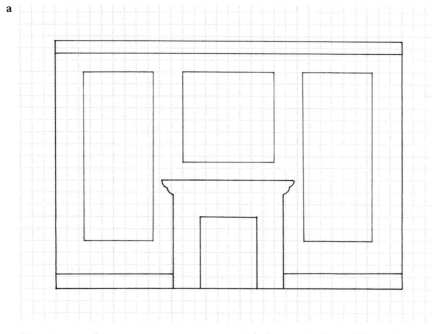

Hanging panels

1 If you are working out the panel size and position on squared paper, calculate the measurements of each panel using your chosen scale (for example, each square = 10cm/6in). Include the measurements between the panels and those between panels and floor/ceiling (**a**).

2 Mark the positions of the panels on the wall, following the plan. Start with the top horizontal line, using a straight edge and spirit level (see page 162) for accuracy. Then mark the verticals with a plumb line (see page 162). If you are marking the position of decorative filler paper, you only need mark one vertical. Lastly, mark the bottom horizontal.

3 If you are using a decorative filler inside the borders, cut this to size first. Use a set square and straight edge to ensure 90° angles on the corners. Paste the panel to the wall, according to the horizontal lines and butting the plumb line (**b**).

4 When the panels are hung, add the border strips using one of the methods suggested on page 177 to mitre the corners.

5 If you are making a panel with a border that has a large repeat, it will not be possible to get all the corners

matching evenly. Make sure that the top corners are perfect as these are the most noticeable. Before cutting the border strips to length, select the joining point on one strip of border and mark and trim the diagonal edge with a transparent set square (**c**).

Position the edge over the adjacent strip at the joining point (**d**) and lightly mark the angle. Then paste the border to the wall, sliding it into position and adjusting it until the motifs match perfectly.

If you are placing prints within the space, these are stuck down after the border, but their positions should first be carefully planned on the squared paper and then marked on the wall.

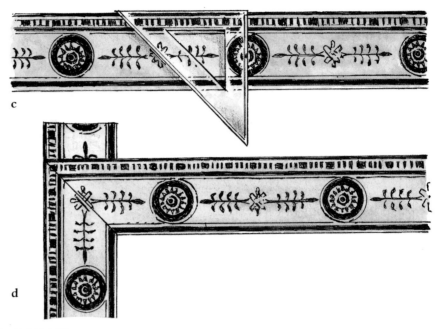

c

d

HANGING CUT-OUT DECORATIONS

If an arrangement is fairly complicated carefully measure it out on the wall, and position it temporarily with Blu-tack. This gives you a chance to check it before pasting. Mark the positions lightly with pencil or use the temporarily stuck pieces as a guide for positioning, as you paste each motif.

Decorative focal points
To make a decorative arrangement like the one over the fireplace on page 111, experiment first to find the best positions for the separate elements. Hang the pieces with Blu-tack and mark their position lightly in pencil. Paste each piece in place, starting with the larger ones. Cover joins with bows, rosettes or knots.

If a rope or ribbon is to look as though it supports a wall-hung object, such as a picture or plate, mark the position of that object first. A single piece can be cut to appear above and below the plate or picture (**e**); it need not continue behind it.

Ceiling decorations
Exact mathematical precision is not essential, as you will seldom look straight up at the ceiling, but a formal arrangement does depend greatly on symmetry for its effectiveness. Mark the centre point of the ceiling, as described for mitring a striped ceiling on page 175, and use this as a guide for positioning.

Hanging columns
Symmetry and accuracy are important, so measure and mark the wall carefully, using a metre rule, set square, spirit level or plumb line as appropriate. Columns can be shortened as required by cutting out a section and rejoining. When pasting the column to the wall, begin at the top and work downwards.

Pasting
Use a good quality wallpaper paste or border adhesive. Cover each piece generously and evenly and allow to soak for five minutes before applying it to the wall.

Intricately shaped pieces are very fragile when wet and should be handled with great care to avoid tearing. Once applied to the wall, however, they can be repositioned with a gentle sliding movement. Smooth them down with a clean cloth, roll the edges firmly with a seam roller and wipe off any excess paste using a damp cloth.

When pasting prints directly to the wall the best adhesive is a starch

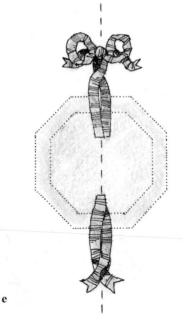

e

paste. A border adhesive may be suitable, but if it is too wet the paper may buckle; a dry spray-mount will give a flat finish but the corners may begin to peel after a time. Experiment with different pastes to find the one that works best with the thickness of your paper. Photocopies on a thin paper may need to be mounted on a light card before pasting, so that they do not crumple and crease when hung.

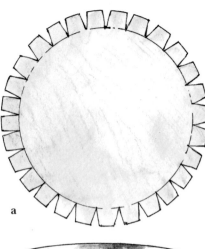

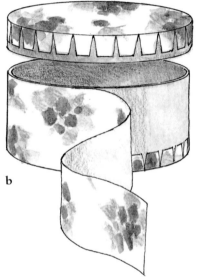

a

b

DECORATIVE ACCESSORIES

Wallpapers as well as other beautiful papers and printed motifs can be used to decorate everyday objects. Working on a small scale allows you to experiment and gain confidence before moving on to more ambitious projects.

To cover a round box

1 Using the base as a template, draw a circle on the wrong side of the paper. Draw a second circle, 2cm/1in larger, round the first. This can be done freehand.

2 Cut wedge-shaped sections round the edge, just short of the inner line (**a**). Paste the piece to the base, sticking each wedge into place on the sides. Repeat this process for the lid, using the lid as a template.

3 Cut a strip the exact depth of the box and as long as the circumference plus 1cm/½in. Paste this to the side of the box (**b**). Repeat for the lid. For the edge of this you may wish to use a contrasting or decorative border.

4 Alternatively, you may decide to continue the paper covering the lid over the edge and down its side. In this case the distance between the outer and inner circles (see Step **1** above), should equal the depth of the lid. Snip all round the edge, up to the inner line, at short intervals (**c**). Paste the piece to the lid, neatly overlapping the snipped flaps on the side (**d**).

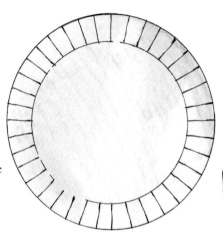

c

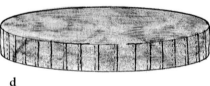

d

To cover a rectangular box

1 Cut pieces for the bottom and lid of the box, adding 1cm/½in all round.

2 Mark the position of the box corners lightly with a pencil, and cut diagonally across them (**e**).

3 Paste the pieces to the box and lid, folding the edges over the sides.

4 Cut the long sides for both box and lid, adding 2cm/1in to the length measurement. The width should fit exactly. Paste the sides in place, overlapping 1cm/½in over at each end (**f**).

5 Cut the short sides, making them fractionally shorter in length than the actual size, and paste them accurately over the ends of the box.

The box can be further embellished with a panel made of narrow border strips or with cut-out motifs.

e

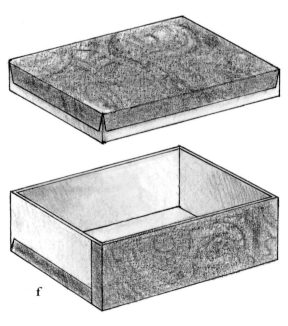

f

Lining cupboards & shelves

To line the inside of a cupboard:

The door

The method is basically the same as for ordinary paperhanging. Make sure that the edges are firmly pasted down, and do not catch when the door is opened. To prevent this, cut the paper fractionally within the edge.

The inside

1 First line the back. Measure the height and width, and cut lengths of wallpaper to these measurements, plus 1cm/½in either side, top and bottom. Paste it to the back of the cupboard, pressing the excess paper into the angles and clipping it at the corners (**g**).

2 Measure the top and bottom and cut lengths of wallpaper to these measurements, adding 2.5cm/1in to the width. You may position the paper across the cupboard or from front to back, depending on which direction shows the pattern to best advantage.

Paste the top and bottom pieces in place, pressing the excess into the angles (**h**).

3 Cut the side pieces to fit exactly. Paste them in position, thus covering the overlaps (**i**).

If the cupboard has shelves, treat each compartment separately.

Shelves

If you are just lining a shelf, cut the paper the width of the shelf but 7.5cm/3in longer than its depth, from front to back. Turn 2.5cm/1in over at the back of the shelf and 5cm/2in over the front. Paste the lining in place.

A kitchen shelf lining should not be pasted down, as you will want to change the paper when it becomes spoilt. It can be held in position with double-sided adhesive tape.

Drawers

If you just wish to line the bottom of the drawer, cut a piece of paper to the exact width of the drawer and 5cm/2in longer than its depth. Fold it under at front and back.

To line the entire drawer, cut pieces as described for covering a rectangular box and paste them to the inside in the same order.

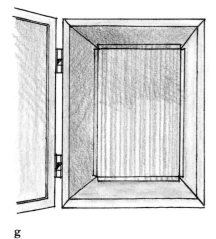

g

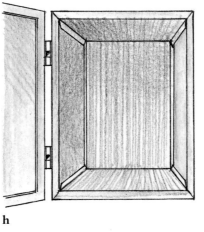

h

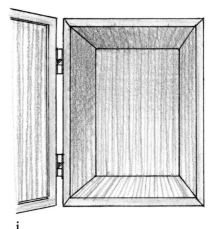

i

Découpage

1 Seal the motifs (whether colour-printed or hand-coloured) with an acrylic spray or a mixture of equal parts white shellac and methylated spirits, applied with a brush.

2 Prepare the object to which the motifs will be applied. Make sure that it is smooth and clean; sand any rough spots. You may wish then to paint or stain the surface. When the object is dry, apply sealer to the surface.

3 Cut out the motifs carefully, using scissors or a scalpel. Begin with the spaces near the centre and work outwards. In delicate, widely spaced areas leave a 'bridge' of white paper (**j**); this is cut away immediately before the motif is glued in place.

4 Apply glue evenly to the back of each motif, and position it on the surface. Press it in place gently but firmly with a barely damp sponge. Make sure that all edges are well stuck down, and remove any excess glue with a cotton bud.

5 Let the object dry overnight; apply another coat of sealer over the entire surface, and let this dry overnight also.

6 Apply 12 or more coats of semigloss varnish, working in a dust-free room and allowing each coat to dry thoroughly (about 24 hours).

7 Between each coat sand the surface with fine wet and dry sandpaper, used wet. Be very careful not to sand down as far as the paper.

8 To finish, go over the surface with good-quality furniture polish applied with a soft, clean cloth.

j

Trompe l'oeil library wallpaper

BIBLIOGRAPHY

Beard, Geoffrey *Craftsmen and Interior Decoration in England 1660–1820* Holmes and Meier, New York 1981

Bredif, Josette *Printed French Fabrics: Toiles de Jouy* Rizzoli, New York 1989

Cornforth, John *The Inspiration of the Past* Viking, London 1985

Entwisle, E.A. *The Book of Wallpaper* Kingsmead, London 1954

Fowler, John and Cornforth, John *English Decoration in the Eighteenth Century* State Mutual Book and Periodical Services, New York 1981

Greysmith, Brenda *Wallpaper* Studio Vista, London 1976

Jacqué, Bernard *Le Papier Peint: Décor d'Illusion* Florilege Gyss Editeurs, Rixheim 1989

Jones, Chester *Colefax & Fowler: The Best in English Interior Decoration* Little, Brown & Co, New York 1989

Jones, Owen *The Grammar of Ornament* Crown, New York 1986

Lynn, Catherine *Wallpaper in America* A Barra Foundation/Cooper-Hewitt Museum Book, W.W. Norton & Company, New York 1980

McClelland, Nancy *Historical Wallpapers* J.B. Lippincott, Philadelphia 1924

Nouvel-Kammerer, Odile *Papiers Peints Français 1800–1850* Office du Livre, Paris 1981
— *Papiers Peints Panoramiques* Musée des Arts Décoratifs/Flammarion, Paris 1990

Nylander, Richard C. *Wallpapers for Historic Buildings* The Preservation Press, Washington, DC 1984

Nylander, Richard C., Redmond, Elizabeth and Sander, Penny J. *Wallpaper in New England* Society for the Preservation of New England Antiquities, Boston, Mass. 1986

Oman, Charles C. and Hamilton, Jean *Wallpapers* Harry Abrams, New York 1982

Teynac, Francoise, Nolot, Pierre and Vivien, Jean-Denis *Wallpaper, A History* Thames & Hudson, Paris 1981

Thornton, Peter *Authentic Decor: The Domestic Interior 1620–1920* Viking Penguin, New York 1984

Turner, Mark and Hoskins, Lesley *Silver Studio of Design* Webb & Bower, London 1988

Victoria & Albert Color Books *Ornate Wallpapers* Harry Abrams, New York 1986

SUPPLIERS

Not all the following companies have showrooms or deal direct with the public. It is always advisable to telephone first for details of your nearest stockist.

Laura Ashley Designer Collection
714 Madison Avenue
New York

1-800-223-6917

G.P. & J. Baker Ltd
PO Box 30
West End Road
High Wycombe
Buckinghamshire HP11 8QD
United Kingdom

0494-71155

Alexander Beauchamp
Available at Christopher Hyland, Inc
D & D Building
979 Third Avenue
New York 10022

(212) 688-6121

Bradbury & Bradbury Art Wallpapers
PO Box 155
Benicia, CA 94510

(707) 746-1900

By appointment San Francisco
(415) 922–2989

Brunschwig & Fils
D & D Building
979 Third Avenue
New York 10022

(212) 838–7878

Rupert Cavendish
Available at Christopher Hyland, Inc
D & D Building
979 Third Avenue
New York 10022

(212) 688-6121

Clarence House
211 East 58th St
New York 10022

(212) 752-2890

Cole & Son
Available at Clarence House
D & D Building
979 Third Avenue
New York 10022

(212) 752-2890

Colefax & Fowler
Available at Cowtan & Tout

Coleman Brothers
Station Approach
Windmill Lane
Cheshunt
Hertfordshire EN8 9AX
United Kingdom

0992-32533

Cowtan & Tout
D & D Building
979 Third Avenue
New York 10022

(212) 753-4488

The Design Archives
North Street
Langley Mill
Nottingham NG16 4BT
United Kingdom

0773-712277

Designers Guild
Available at Osborne & Little, Inc

Dovedale Fabrics Ltd
Caerphilly Road
Ystrad Mynach
Hengoed
Mid Glamorgan CF8 78P
United Kingdom

0443-815520

De Gournay
41 Brompton Square
London SW3 2AF
United Kingdom

071 823-7316

Grammage
Papers available through M. E. Short Ltd

Hamilton Weston Wallpapers Ltd
Available at Christopher Hyland, Inc
D & D Building
979 Third Avenue
New York 10022

(212) 688-6121

S. Harris & Co
D & D Building
979 Third Avenue
New York 10022

(212) 838-5253

Irish Georgian Society
Leixlip Castle
Leixlip
County Kildare
Ireland

010 353 16244211

Marybert Creations S.A.R.L.
BP 106-68170
Rixheim
France

010 33 89-652-025

Massacco
17 White Street
New York 10013

(212) 925-8667

Mauny
Papers available through Guy Evans
51a Cleveland St
London W1P 5PQ
United Kingdom

071 436-7914

National Trust (Head Office)
36 Queen Anne's Gate
London SW1
United Kingdom

071 222-9251

Christopher Neville Design
55 Endell St
London WC2
United Kingdom

071 240-5844/-7387

Nobilis-Fontan Ltd
Available at Hines & Co
D & D Building
979 Third Avenue
New York 10022

(212) 685-8590

John S. Oliver Ltd
33 Pembridge Road
London W11 3HG
United Kingdom

071 221-6466/727-3735

Ornamenta
Available at Christopher Hyland, Inc
D & D Building
979 Third Avenue
New York 10022

(212) 688-6121

Osborne & Little, Inc
D & D Building
979 Third Avenue
New York 10022

(212) 751-3333

Pallu & Lake
Available at F. Schumacher & Co

Parkertex Fabrics Ltd
Available through G.P. & J. Baker Ltd

Ramm, Son and Crocker
Chiltern House
Knaves Beech Business Centre
High Wycombe
Buckinghamshire HP10 9QY
United Kingdom

0628-850777

Arthur Sanderson & Sons Ltd
D & D Building
979 Third Avenue
New York 10022

(212) 319-7220

Scalamandré Silks, Inc
950 Third Avenue
New York 10022

(212) 980-7220

F. Schumacher & Co
939 Third Avenue
New York 10022

(212) 415-3900

Muriel Short/M.E. Short Ltd
Unit 2, Hewitts Estate
Elmbridge Road
Cranleigh
Surrey GU6 8LW
United Kingdom

0483-271211

Souleiado
Available at Pierre Deux
870 Madison Avenue
New York 10021

(212) 570-9343

Timney Fowler Ltd
Available at Christopher Hyland, Inc
D & D Building
979 Third Avenue
New York 10021

(212) 688-6121

Today Interiors Ltd
Available through Payne Fabrics
979 Third Avenue
New York 10022

800-543-4322

Warner Fabrics plc
Bradbourne Drive
Tilbrook
Milton Keynes MK7 8BE
United Kingdom

0908-366900

Watts of Westminster
Available at Christopher Hyland, Inc
D & D Building
979 Third Avenue
New York 10021

(212) 688-6121

Nicola Wingate-Saul
Print Rooms
47 Moreton Terrace
London SW1V 2NS
United Kingdom

071 821-1577

Brian Yates (Interiors) Ltd
3 Riverside Park
Carton Road
Lancaster LA1 3PE
United Kingdom

0524 35035

Zoffany Ltd
Some patterns available at
Christopher Lloyd
D & D Building
979 Third Avenue
New York 10021

(212) 688-6121

Zuber & Cie
D & D Building
979 Third Avenue
New York 10021

(212) 486-9226

SUPPLIERS' CREDITS

*Items for special photography
were supplied by the following:*

Pages 10/11 Brunschwig & Fils

Page 12 Zuber & Cie

Page 16 **1, 2** Ornamenta; **3, 4** Zoffany; **5** Colefax & Fowler; **6** Ramm, Son & Crocker; **7, 8, 9** Clarence House; **10** Design Archives

Page 17 **1, 3, 4** Zoffany; **2, 8** Alexander Beauchamp; **5, 9** Sanderson; **6** Cole & Son. **Curtain** Watts of Westminster; **fabric** on chair and stool The Gainsborough Silk Weaving Co, Alexandra Road, Chilton, Sudbury, Suffolk CO10 6XH (0787 72081)

Page 21 **1** Nobilis-Fontan; **2, 3** G.P. & J. Baker; **4** Cole & Son; **5** Zoffany;

6 Schumacher. **Antique toile curtain** Christopher Moore at The Lacy Gallery, 38 Ledbury Road, London W11 (071 792 3628)

Page 23 **Background wallpapers** Nobilis-Fontan (left); Parkertex (right). **Wallpapers on chair and floor** Alexander Beauchamp

Page 25 John Oliver

Page 26 **Wallpaper and wall decorations** Ornamenta; **prints** ARC, 26 North Street, London SW4 0HB (071 720 1628); **flooring** Crucial Trading, PO Box 689, London W2 4BX (071 727 3634); **curtains, cushions and wall sconces** Colefax & Fowler; **antique chairs and tablecloth** Valerie Wade, 108 Fulham Road, London SW3 6HS (071 225 1414);

Gothick planter Town & Country Conservatories, 8 & 9 Murray Street, London NW1 (071 267 7050)

Page 27 **1, 2** Brunschwig & Fils; **3, 4, 5** Alexander Beauchamp. **Stone floor** Stone Age, 67 Dendy Street, London SW12 8DA (081 673 7284)

Page 29 **1** Brunschwig & Fils; **2** Brian Yates; **all other wallpapers** Nobilis-Fontan. **Table** Pineapple, Clevedon Cottages, Clevedon Works, off London Street, Bath (0225 446181)

Page 37 **Chinese wallpaper** Zoffany

Page 46 Cole & Son

Page 50 (left) Colefax & Fowler

Page 51 (right) Colefax & Fowler

Pages 54/5 Zoffany

Page 56 **Top to bottom** Colefax & Fowler; Ornamenta; Colefax & Fowler; Mauny; Zoffany; Colefax & Fowler; Zoffany; Mauny; Brunschwig & Fils; Hamilton Weston; Laura Ashley

Page 65 **Wallpaper, border and textiles** Souleiado

Page 66 **Top to bottom** Mauny; Nobilis-Fontan; Hamilton Weston; Zoffany; Ornamenta; Muriel Short; Osborne & Little; Alexander Beauchamp; Rupert Cavendish

Page 67 **Top to bottom** Scalamandré; Osborne & Little; Zoffany; Schumacher; Osborne & Little; Cole & Son; Laura Ashley, Massacco; Brunschwig & Fils

Page 70 **Top to bottom** Ornamenta; Nobilis-Fontan; Brunschwig & Fils; Warner

Page 71 **Top to bottom** Mauny; Mauny; Brunschwig & Fils; Rupert Cavendish; Mauny

Page 72 **Top row, left to right** Muriel Short; Nobilis-Fontan; Mauny; Colefax & Fowler. **Bottom row, left to right** Colefax & Fowler; Mauny; Mauny; Nobilis-Fontan. **Wallpaper** Ornamenta; **curtain poles** Laura Ashley; **ropes and tassels** Wemyss Houlès, 40 Newman Street, London WIP 3PA (071 255 3305)

Page 74 **I** Designers Guild; **2, 4, 8, 9** Laura Ashley; **3, 7** Nobilis-Fontan; **5** Ramm, Son & Crocker; **6, 12** Warner; **10** Sanderson; **II** Mauny

Page 78 **Wallpaper and border** Alexander Beauchamp. **Chandelier** McCloud & Co, 61 Hillier Road, London SWII (071 350 1448)

Page 88 **Left to right: border** Osborne & Little; **wallpaper** Ramm, Son & Crocker; **border and wallpaper** Today Interiors; **border and wallpaper** Zoffany; **border and cornerpiece** Brunschwig & Fils; **wallpaper** Ornamenta

Page 92 **Left to right** Brunschwig & Fils; Brunschwig & Fils; Brian Yates; Mauny

Page 93 **Left to right: border and cornerpiece** Ornamenta; **border and cornerpiece** Laura Ashley; **borders** Colefax & Fowler; **cornerpiece** Cole & Son

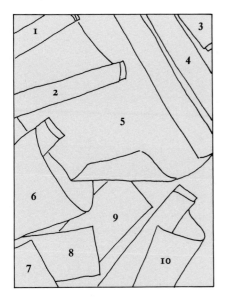

Page 16

Page 17

Page 21

Page 27

Page 29

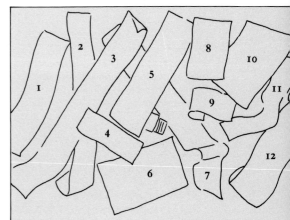

Page 74

Pages 96/7 **Wallpapers** Muriel Short; **border along cornice and skirting board** Rupert Cavendish; **border round panels** Cole & Son. **Prints** ARC (see page 26) and Florentina, 59 High Street, Dorchester on Thames OX10 7HN (0865 340097); **table** Soho Designs Ltd, 263 Kings Road, London SW3 (071 376 5855); **chairs, bust and bowl** Restall, Brown & Clennell, Cosgrove Hall, Cosgrove, Milton Keynes MK19 7JB (0908 565888)

Pages 100/1 **Background wallpaper** Ornamenta; **wallpapers in panels and borders** Laura Ashley Decorator Collection

Page 102 **Background wallpaper** Nobilis-Fontan; **wallpaper forming borders and diamonds** Grammage; **other wallpaper** Pallu & Lake. **Furniture and chandelier** Davies, 10 Great Newport Street, London WC2H 7JA (071 240 2223); **wooden floor** Kahrs UK Ltd, Timber Lane Estate, Quarry Lane, Chichester, W Sussex (0243 778747)

Page 108 **Wall decorations** Ornamenta; Nicholas Gibbs; Cowtan & Tout; Sanderson

Page 110 **Wallpaper and wall decorations** Ornamenta

Page 113 **Wallpaper and wall decorations** Ornamenta. **Chair** Restall, Brown & Clennell (see pages 96/7)

Page 114 **Wallpaper and wall decorations** Ornamenta. **Wicker furniture** Town & Country Conservatories (see page 26); **curtain** Designers Guild; **wooden floor** Kahrs UK Ltd (see page 102); **camel bone balls** Joss Graham, 10 Eccleston Street, London SW1 (071 730 4370)

Page 117 **Dado paper** Alexander Beauchamp

Page 118 **Wallpaper** John Oliver; **columns and balustrades** John Oliver. **Furniture and accessories** Rupert Cavendish; **cushions** Timney Fowler; **flooring** Crucial Trading (see page 26)

Page 119 **Columns** (*left*) Ornamenta, (*right*) Christopher Neville. **Ivy** cut from wallpaper by Sanderson

Page 120 **Overdoor** David Ison

Page 120 **Orange tree** Nobilis-Fontan; **wallpaper** Ornamenta. **Table and**

chair The Monica Pitman Collection, 1 Elystan Place, London SW3 3LA (071 581 1404); **rug** Veronica Marsh, Manor Stables, Higher Eype, Bridport, Dorset DT6 6AT (0308 25958)

Page 122 **Print room borders** Nicola Wingate-Saul; National Trust; Irish Georgian Society; Ornamenta

Page 132 (top) Irish Georgian Society

Page 132 (bottom) National Trust

Page 133 **Border** Osborne & Little; **bow** Ornamenta. **Print** ARC (see page 26)

Page 134 (bottom) **Wall decorations** Ornamenta. **Print** Florentina (see pages 96/7)

Page 135 **Pink wallpaper** Cole & Son; **blue wallpaper** Sanderson; **ribbon border** Laura Ashley; **plain borders** Colefax & Fowler; **wall decorations** Ornamenta

Page 136 **Background wallpaper** Osborne & Little. **Prints** ARC (see page 26) and Florentina (see pages 96/7); **chairs, curtain and tablecloth** Souleiado; **flooring** Crucial Trading (see page 26)

Page 137 **Top to bottom** Cole & Son; Osborne & Little; Cole & Son; Colefax & Fowler; Dovedale; Dovedale; Colefax & Fowler; Dovedale; Colefax & Fowler

Page 140 (bottom) Zuber & Cie

Page 141 **Top left** Waterhouse Wallhangings; **top right** Harris Fabrics; **bottom left** Cole & Son; **bottom right** Brunschwig & Fils

Page 144 **Wallpaper and borders** Laura Ashley; Warner; Ornamenta; Nobilis-Fontan; Cole & Son; Ramm, Son & Crocker; Zoffany. **Mirror** CVP, 27 Bruton Place, London W1 (071 493 7995); **floor** Stone Age (see page 27)

Page 146 **Covered boxes and marbled papers** The Italian Paper Shop, Brompton Arcade, London SW3 (071 589 1668); Compton Marbling, Lower Lawn Barns, Tisbury, Nr Salisbury, Wilts SP3 6SG (0747 871147); **mirror and console table** McCloud & Co (see page 78)

Page 147 **Spice chest** D.R. Coble & Co, PO Box 479, Angola, In 46703, USA (0101 219 665 2448)

Page 148 **Background wallpaper and wallpapers covering boxes** Timney Fowler; **chair** by Piero Fornasetti from Oggetti, 100 Jermyn Street, London SW1 (071 930 4694); **flooring** Amtico, 17 St George Street, London W1R 9DE (071 629 6258); **portfolios** private collection

Page 150 Pine chest lined with wallpaper from Alexander Beauchamp

Page 150 **Top to bottom** Alexander Beauchamp; Cole & Son; Alexander Beauchamp; Sanderson

Page 151 **Découpage bedhead** Jane Gordon-Smith, Yew Glen House, Castle Street, Mere, Wilts BA12 6JE (0747 860865)

Page 152 **Boxes** Nicola Wingate-Saul

Page 154 (top) **Wallpaper** Sanderson; **silhouette frames** Raynham Workshops, 8 Eccleston Street, London SW1 (071 730 8287)

Page 155 **Top screen** Ornamenta; **bottom screen** P & R Decorative Arts, The Parlour, Grove Farm, Grove Lane, Chesham, Bucks HP5 3QQ (0494 785355)

Page 159 **1, 3** Woolpit Interiors, The Street, Woolpit, Bury St Edmunds, Suffolk IP30 9SA (0359 40895); **2, 4** Susan M. Foster, The Keeping Room, 124 Delaware Street, New Castle De 19720, USA (0101 302 328 7125). **5, 7, 8** Acres Farm Fenders, Acres Farm, Bradfield, Berks RG7 6JH (0734 744305); **6** Charlotte Smith Designs, 20 Station Hill, Swimbridge, North Devon (0271 830713). **Lamp bases** from Acres Farm Fenders and Charlotte Smith Designs

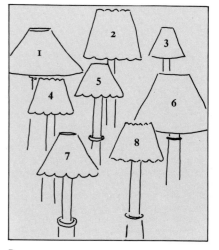

Page 159

Editor Anne Kilborn **Design** Anne Wilson
Picture Editor Anne Fraser **Picture Researcher** Sue Gladstone

Photographer Tim Imrie **Styling** Jane Gordon-Clark, Anne Wilson
Illustrator Jim Robins

Editorial Director Erica Hunningher **Associate Art Directors** Tim Foster, Caroline Hillier
Production Director Nicky Bowden

AUTHOR'S ACKNOWLEDGMENTS

The production of this book has been a rewarding and challenging experience.

At the beginning, in the research stages, several museum curators and librarians generously gave me the benefit of their time and experience or pointed me in the right direction for further study. In France Bernard Jacqué at the Musée du Papier Peint in Rixheim and Véronique de Bruignac at the Musée des Arts Décoratifs in Paris kindly showed me part of their comprehensive wallpaper collections. Most helpful also were Crosby Forbes at the Peabody Museum of Salem, Massachusetts, Elizabeth Padjen, Richard Nylander at the S.P.N.E.A. in Boston, Massachusetts, Heather Wood at the Royal Pavilion in Brighton, the staff of the wallpaper collection at the Victoria and Albert Museum in London, the curators of many National Trust properties and the owners of historic houses containing beautiful antique wallpapers.

Many people in the world of interior design were enthusiastic and encouraging about the project and I would especially like to thank Anthony Evans of Top Layer, George Toynbee-Clarke of Toynbee-Clarke Interiors, Trudy Ballard of Colefax & Fowler, Norman Gibbon of Arthur Sanderson & Sons Ltd, Judith Straeten of Brunschwig & Fils, New York and Cleo Carnelli at Nobilis-Fontan in Paris. Helpful technical advice was given by Frank Burtenshaw at Hampshire Prints, Ron Davidson at Designers Wallpaper Company, Denis Hall at John Perry Wallpapers, and Karen Beauchamp of Alexander Beauchamp.

Several friends kindly lent objects and furniture for photography or allowed us to photograph their houses. Among them I should particularly like to thank Victoria Faulkner, Nicola Crawley, Tom Faulkner and Kate Buckett. Special thanks are due to Matilda Bathurst whose organizational abilities ensured the smooth running of both the photography and the office. Tim Imrie, the photographer, always responded with imagination and originality to our suggestions. Annabel Jones Lloyd and Rebecca Bothway tackled the endless typing with good natured patience.

I should particularly like to thank Frances Lincoln for the original idea for *Paper Magic* and her positive support as the project developed. Especially vital was the creative inspiration of the designer Anne Wilson, and the untiring enthusiasm of the editor Anne Kilborn, both of whose expertise was so generously given. Eleanor Van Zandt, Penny David, Anne Fraser, Sue Gladstone and Sallie Coolidge also contributed skills and hard work which was greatly appreciated.

Charlotte, Venetia, Fenella, Matthew and Sam I thank for their forebearance when submerged for months by wallpaper samples, and for never failing to give good-humoured and enthusiastic encouragement.

PUBLISHERS' ACKNOWLEDGMENTS

Frances Lincoln Publishers thank the many companies who generously loaned items for special photography and the people who kindly allowed their rooms to be photographed, particularly Nicola Wingate-Saul Print Rooms, Top Layer and François Gilles and Dominique Lubar from I.P.L. Interiors. The Directors of Coutts & Co are gratefully acknowledged for allowing us to photograph the Chinese panorama at their headquarters.

Special thanks to Tim Imrie for his hard work and good humour, to Jo Miesikowski and Andy Font for their help with studio photography and to Sue Gladstone for her imaginative pursuit of pictorial material. For their speed and cheerful cooperation we thank Servis Filmsetting Ltd, and particularly Alan Rayner.

PHOTOGRAPHIC CREDITS

t=top   *l*=left
b=bottom *r*=right

All pictures by Tim Imrie, © Frances Lincoln Limited except:

Agence Top/Joseph Schnapp 41; Peter Aprahamian 68, 138, 155*l*; ARCAID/Richard Bryant 53, 63*b*, 156; Mark Fiennes 15; Lucinda Lambton 34, 36, 63*l*; Julie Phipps 157; Robert Benson 6, 38, 62, 75*t*; Boys Syndication/Michael Boys 19, 63*tr*; Bracken Books, London 52; Brunschwig & Fils: 7, 23*t*, 39*tr*, 184; Nick Carter 91, 99; Castletown Foundation Ltd 128; D.R. Coble and Company 147*b*; Cole & Son (Wallpapers) Ltd 8; Coleman Bros/ Valentino 7 Collection 85; Courtesy of the Cooper-Hewitt Museum, Smithsonian Institution/Art Resource, NY/Scott Hyde 145; Denis Davis 141*tl*; Peo Eriksson 35*t*, 58; Glebe Gallery, Co. Donegal/Con Brogan 153*l*; De Gournay 105; Kari Haavisto 31*l*; John Hall 22, 40, 48, 60*l*; Lars Hallen 104; Historisches Museum, Basel/Maurice Babey 103*t*; Marybert Créations S.A.R.L. 6; Derry Moore 14*b*, 24, 51*t*, 75*b*, 125, 129, 131; Collection du Musée des Arts Décoratifs, Paris/photo M.A.D./L. Sully-Jaulmes 98*l*, 107; Nobilis-Fontan Ltd 61*r*, 87*b*, 95*l*, 98*r*; Ornamenta/31*r*, 111, 155*tr*; Paul Ryan/J.B. Visual Press 149; Ianthe Ruthven 42, 124*b*, 127; © Frances Lincoln Limited 28 (designer: IPL Interiors), 59, 65, 139 (Nicola Wingate-Saul print rooms made by Denise Czyrka), 152; Arthur Sanderson and Sons Ltd 61*l*, 84; Fritz von der Schulenburg 43, 49, 50*b*, 147*t*; P & R Decorative Arts 155*b*; By kind permission of Mr and Mrs Peter Smedley 130; Arthur Thomson 151*t*; Victoria & Albert Museum, London (By Courtesy of the Board of Trustees) 35*b*, 80, 82, 87*t*, 140*l*; Elizabeth Whiting & Associates/Andreas von Einsiedel 14*t*; The Whitworth Art Gallery, University of Manchester 86; Peter Woloszynski 30, 77*l*; The World of Interiors: Simon Brown 60*r*, 116; James Mortimer 69, 76, 94; World Press Network Ltd/IPC Magazines 20, 29*t*, 81, 83, 117*t*, 151*b*; Zoffany 39*tl*; Zuber & Cie 140*r*.